S H O R T   W A L K S

CW00369643

Spectacular Side Pike mirrored in the placid waters of Blea Tarn

C E N T R A L   &   S O U T H   L A K E   D I S T R I C T

Central & Southern Lake District

CONTENTS

EXPLANATION OF
DEGREE OF DIFFICULTY:
1: Very Easy, 2: Easy, 3: Easy, 4: Easy to Moderate, 5: Moderate, 6: Moderate, 7: Moderate to Strenuous, 8: Strenuous, 9: Strenuous, 10: Extremely Strenuous.

IMPORTANT: Please note that these gradings and the time lengths quoted below are based on the personal experience of the author and may vary significantly between individual walkers

WALKED AND WRITTEN BY JOHN WATSON.
SERIES CONCEPT AND DESIGN: MALCOLM PARKER.
ARTWORK AND DESIGN: RACHEL PAXTON
& ANDREW FALLON.

PUBLISHED BY WALKS OF DISCOVERY LTD.,
1 MARKET PLACE, MIDDLETON-IN-TEESDALE.
CO. DURHAM, DL12 0QG. TEL: (01833) 640638.

PRINTED IN ENGLAND. ISBN 0-86309-132-6.
COPYRIGHT © WALKS OF DISCOVERY LIMITED 1996.

Central & Southern Lake District

CONTENTS

How to use this Guide

This guide is designed to be used by walkers who have some experience, are appropriately dressed and equipped, and are able to interpret Ordnance Survey Maps.

■ **1 CHOOSE YOUR ROUTE** Study the general location map opposite indicating our selection of 18 walk routes, then consult their individual route summary, route description and route map before making your personal choice. Each 'circular' walk starts and finishes at the same point for your convenience.

■ **2 CHECK THE ROUTE SUITABILITY** Carefully study your selected route to ensure that it is suitable for you, but particularly the weakest member of your party. To do this also consider the grading system for length and degree of difficulty for each route on the contents pages - as well as the information detailed on each individual walk description.

■ **3 CHECK THE WEATHER CONDITIONS** Before you set out it is essential that you check the current and developing weather conditions. In addition, you should consider the Walking and Safety Tips on pages 64 and 65. Also be aware of the telephone numbers of the emergency services.

■ **4 USE WITH AN ORDNANCE SURVEY MAP** This guide is designed to be used with the relevant 1:25 000 and 1:50 000 scale O.S. Maps of the area should you so wish. Grid references are used in the guide.

■ **5 USING THE MAP AND ROUTE DESCRIPTION TOGETHER** This guide is designed so that the route map and route description can be easily used together with the relevant 1:25 000 Ordnance Survey Map should you so wish. The detailed, concise route descriptions are clearly numbered in both the text and on the route map to help you locate your position.

The shores of expansive Coniston Water

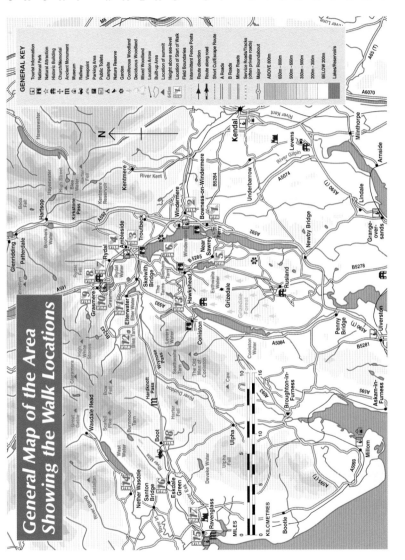

General Map of the Area
Showing the Walk Locations

GENERAL KEY

- Tourist Information
- National Park
- Natural Attraction
- Historic Building
- Church/Memorial
- Ancient Monument
- Museum
- Railway
- Viewpoint
- Parking Area
- Public Toilets
- Campsite
- Nature Reserve
- Garden
- Coniferous Woodland
- Deciduous Woodland
- Mixed Woodland
- Built-up Area
- Location Arrow
- Location of summit
- Height above sea-level
- Location of Start of Walk
- Intermittent Fence Posts
- Field Boundaries
- Route direction
- Route along road
- Short Cut/Escape Route
- A Roads
- B Roads
- Minor Roads
- Service Roads/Tracks (often private roads)
- Major Roundabout
- ABOVE 600m
- 650m – 800m
- 500m – 650m
- 350m – 500m
- 200m – 350m
- BELOW 200m
- Lakes/Reservoirs

Summary of all 18 Walks

■ **WALK 1: Bowness-on-Windermere**
The bustle of this lakeside town is soon exchanged for a peaceful rural hinterland characterised by meadows, woodland glades, leafy lanes and open fell. This pastoral landscape lies between Biskey Howe and Post Knott, high points with panoramic views over Windermere to the central fells.

■ **WALK 2: Orrest Head** Busy Windermere is left behind on a short climb beneath a woodland canopy onto the airy heights of Orrest Head, a renowned Lakeland viewpoint. The lake below is backed by a skyline etched with pinnacles of the central fells. The return stroll is via fields, lanes and woods.

■ **WALK 3: Stockghyll Force** It is close to the centre of Ambleside, reached by a riverbank walk up a wooded gorge. The falls are spectacular whether viewed from below or from the bridge over their head. Once out of the ravine, open countryside along lanes and over meadowland affords views of the fells beyond.

■ **WALK 4: Sweden Bridges** From Ambleside a walled path cuts up between fields and woods into the foothills of the high fells. Humpbacked High Sweden Bridge is a remote scenic turning-point for a grassy descent to picturesque Low Sweden Bridge and its waterfalls, with views over Ambleside and Windermere lake throughout.

■ **WALK 5: The Sawreys** A popular National Trust property is Beatrix Potter's cottage, Hill Top, at Near Sawrey. Views over lake and tarn, quiet lanes, meadows, woodland and the quaint hamlets of Near and Far Sawrey on this easy walk no doubt served as an inspiration to the imagination of the world-famous authoress.

■ **WALK 6: Blelham Tarn** A terraced meadowland and woodland circuit of tiny secluded Blelham Tarn, a National Nature Reserve, leads to the rocky cove of High Wray Bay on Windermere lake and the attractive wooded grounds of Wray Castle, a mock medieval C19th house, not open to the public.

■ **WALK 7: Rydal Water** A circular walk round the lower fells, which enclose Rydal Water, provides superb aerial aspects of the lake and glimpses of its neighbour, Grasmere. These views inspired the poetry of William Wordsworth whose home at Rydal Mount can be visited en route. Cathedral-like Rydal Cave is also a fascinating attraction.

■ **WALK 8: Alcock Tarn** This minuscule tarn is perched high on a mountain plateau. Ascent and descent paths are quite steep, but frequent rest-stops are rewarded with panoramic views over the vale of Grasmere to the central fells and over Windermere to Morecambe Bay. William Wordsworth's early home, Dove Cottage, can be visited en route.

■ **WALK 9: Easedale Tarn** 'My heart leaps up when I behold a rainbow in the sky'. So wrote Wordsworth by Easedale Tarn, cloistered high in its mountain setting at the geographical centre of the

Lake District. Water dominates a walk upstream in Far Easedale valley to the tarn and downstream beside the cascading falls of Sourmilk Gill.

■ **WALK 10: Helm Crag** High above Grasmere, Helm Crag's shapely summit has earned for it such titles as 'The Lion and The Lamb' and 'The Lady at the Organ'. This magnificent rocky viewpoint is achieved on a gradual climb via lane, field, stream, waterfall, fell and undulating ridge - a mountain experience with minimum effort.

■ **WALK 11: Elter Water** From the meadows fringing the reeded shoreline of this swan lake, for 'Elter' is Norse for 'swan', is a classic view of the Langdale Pikes, only one scenic aspect of a walk over rolling hills, along tumbling streams and through shaded woodland, plus an encounter with two plunging waterfalls.

■ **WALK 12: Blea Tarn** Between Great and Little Langdale, romantic little Blea Tarn nestles in an upland hollow protected by surrounding mountains. Like the Langdale Pikes, it is rarely out of sight on a walk which touches its shoreline, and after a short steep climb is viewed from on high along a fine heather moorland ridge.

■ **WALK 13: Tarn Hows** One of Lakeland's most popular beauty spots, the route seeks solitude away from the often crowded shoreline by keeping above the tarn which also enhances the views. Tree-fringed waterfalls up Glen Mary prepare the way for the magic of the tarn and glorious panoramic views from the ridge of Tom Heights.

■ **WALK 14: Wast Water** Tiny Flass Tarn, couched in farmland contrasts

with the dark waters of England's deepest lake, Wast Water, set against a towering wall of scree and England's highest mountains, the Scafells and Great Gable, at its head. Between, lie meadows, sylvan banks of the River Irt, and a return over low fell.

■ **WALK 15: Muncaster Castle** An easy climb from the ancient port of Ravenglass, past a Roman bath-house and through woodland, emerges at C14th Muncaster Castle, later a Victorian country house. The walk through its landscaped gardens is followed by a grassland descent to the beach of the Esk estuary.

■ **WALK 16: Miterdale** A gradual ascent of peaceful Miterdale follows the River Mite to Burnmoor Tarn, set amidst open fell below Scafell Pike, England's highest mountain. A descent into Boot village follows an old corpse path. Return is by train on a narrow-gauge track along the delightful Esk Valley.

■ **WALK 17: Muncaster Fell** Fell Lane, once part of Britain's highest Roman road over the Lake District, climbs gently onto Hooker Crag with sea views. The fell top is crossed on a sinuous path into Eskdale. A narrow-gauge railway journey to working Muncaster Mill, plus a short woodland climb to Muncaster Castle, ends the walk.

■ **WALK 18: Stanley Force** A path up Stanley Gill in a wooded ravine leads to a dramatic waterfall. Back at the bottom of the gorge, the tumbling tree-fringed River Esk, backed by distant fells, is traced to a picturesque packhorse bridge for a return along the opposite riverbank.

WALK 1

BOWNESS-ON-WINDERMERE - SCHOOL KNOTT - POST KNOTT

4.5 MILES (7.2 km)

Route Details

Distance	4.5 miles (7.2 km)
Degree of Difficulty	Easy
Ascent	120m (394ft)
Time	3 hours

Start and Finish Points

National Trust car park, Rayrigg Road Bowness-on-Windermere (GR 402971). It is situated off the A592, south-west from Penrith via Ullswater and north from Newby Bridge along the eastern shore of Windermere.

Maps Needed

OS Outdoor Leisure No 7 (1:25 000)
OS Landranger No 96 (1:50 000)

Parking Facilities

The National Trust pay and display Rayrigg Road car park (GR 402971) is centrally placed in Bowness-on-Windermere with easy access to all the facilities of this small, busy town. Should the car park be full, three other car parks are situated a short distance south of the town centre and close to the lakeshore.

Route Description

■ **1** Start at the car park entrance. Cross the road. Turn right.

■ **2** Double back left round The Albert public house at a roundabout. Go up the Windermere road for 75m.

■ **3** Turn right to cross the road. Go straight up Helm Road opposite. Pass the Hydro Hotel on the left.

Detour: At (4) proceed to a sharp right-hand bend. Turn left up steps adjacent to a lamppost. Go ahead to the Biskey Howe viewpoint. Return to (4).

■ **4** Go ahead up a tarmac lane. Ignore references to cul-de-sac and private. Go between stone gate pillars signed to Helm Farm. Bear right at a fork along a lane. Arrive at Helm Farm cottage (built 1691) on the right.

■ **5** Turn left through a kissing-gate where the lane bends sharply right. Follow a field path. Go through a kissing-gate. Continue to the end of the path and through a stepped wall gap. Proceed for 15m.

■ **6** Turn right on a narrow path with a high box hedge on the left. Enter woodland with garden hedges and houses on the left.

■ **7** Turn sharp right where four paths meet at a signpost with three paths

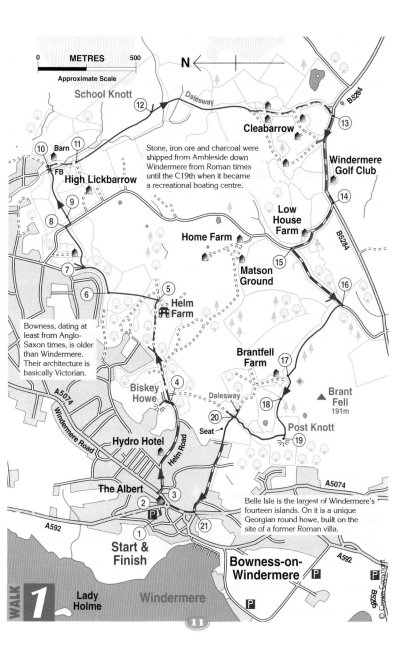

METRES 0 — 500
Approximate Scale

N ←

School Knott

Dalesway

(12)

(10) Barn (11)
FB
High Lickbarrow

(9)

(8)

(7)

(6)

(5) Helm Farm

Bowness, dating at least from Anglo-Saxon times, is older than Windermere. Their architecture is basically Victorian.

Biskey Howe

(4)

Dalesway

Hydro Hotel

Helm Road

The Albert

(2)
P
(3)

(1)

Start & Finish

Lady Holme

Windermere

Stone, iron ore and charcoal were shipped from Ambleside down Windermere from Roman times until the C19th when it became a recreational boating centre.

Cleabarrow

(13)

Windermere Golf Club

(14)

B5284

Low House Farm

Home Farm

(15)

Matson Ground

(16)

Brantfell Farm

(17)

Brant Fell 191m

(18)

(20)
Seat

(19)
Post Knott

A5074

Belle Isle is the largest of Windermere's fourteen islands. On it is a unique Georgian round howe, built on the site of a former Roman villa.

(21)

Bowness-on-Windermere P
P

A592

B5284

A5074

A592

© Crown Copyright

WALK
1

Windermere Road

A5074

indicating Windermere. Climb a narrow path through trees. The path meanders high along a bankside. Pass through a kissing-gate at a house on the left. Continue ahead over meadowland. Pass through a kissing-gate adjacent to a field-gate. Emerge onto a road.

■ **8** Turn right on the road. Turn left after 10m. Cross the road. Pass over a stone-stepped stile into a field.

■ **9** Cross the field along a wall on the right. At the wall corner, cut diagonally across the field to join another wall. Pass over a ladder-stile at the bottom corner of the field. Immediately cross a footbridge. Climb steps onto a lane.

■ **10** Turn right along the lane, passing a barn on the left.

■ **11** Where the lane bends sharply right go straight ahead through a field-gate. Proceed on a broad path through another field-gate. Ford a shallow stream. Gradually traverse the lower slopes of School Knott up on the left.

■ **12** Bear right, downhill, at a fork on the Dalesway footpath. Pass through three field-gates. Go between two houses. The path becomes a tarmac walled lane with a small tarn over to the left.

■ **13** Turn right onto the B5284. Go along the road, passing the junction with the Dalesway footpath on the right and Windermere Golf Club on the left.

■ **14** Turn right, off the main road. Go along a minor road signposted to Heathwaite.

■ **15** Turn left at a junction onto another minor road signposted to Bowness. Proceed for 350m to a depression in the road.

■ **16** Turn right at the second of two signposts which are 30m apart. Cross over a stile adjacent to a field-gate.

Follow a broad path which bends left, contouring round the lower slopes of Brant Fell up on the left.

■ **17** Go up left at a ground-level footpath sign just before Brantfell Farm. Follow round the external wall of the farm on the right. Cross over a stile. Go ahead on a downhill path along the wall on the right. Pass over a stone stile at the bottom of the path.

■ **18** Bear left on a path bending right across meadowland. Aim for the highest rocky promontory of Post Knott.

The upper reaches of Windermere from Biskey Howe

■ **19** Turn right, downhill, from the summit. Pass through a kissing-gate adjacent to a field-gate into woodland. Go down a clear winding path.

■ **20** Turn left through a kissing-gate adjacent to a field-gate at a footpath sign immediately before two gateposts at cross-paths. Go down the hillside on the Dalesway footpath, passing a stone slab seat. Pass through a wicket-gate adjacent to a field-gate at the bottom of the slope. Go straight ahead down a road into the centre of Bowness.

■ **21** Turn right at the junction with the main road. Go along a one-way street to the roundabout at (2). Follow the outward route back to the car park.

WALK 2

WINDERMERE TOWN - ELLERAY WOOD - ORREST HEAD - HIGH HAY WOOD
3.1 MILES (5 km)

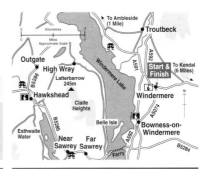

Route Details

Distance	3.1 miles (5 km)
Degree of Difficulty	Easy
Ascent	248m (813ft)
Time	2.5 hours

Start and Finish Points

Broad Street car park, Windermere town centre (GR 414982).
On the A591, from Ambleside, turn right into Windermere onto the A5074 just before the station on the right.
From Kendal, on the A591, turn left onto the A5074 at Windermere Station. Follow the parking signs into Broad Street on the left.

Maps Needed

OS Outdoor Leisure No 7 (1:25 000)
OS Landranger No 90 (1:50 000)
OS Landranger No 96 (1:50 000)

Parking Facilities

Broad Street pay and display car park (GR 414982) is large and in the centre of Windermere. There is limited lay-by parking on the A591 going towards Kendal just past the railway station.

Route Description

■ **1** Start from the Broad Street entrance to the car park. Turn left down Broad Street to the junction with the main road.

■ **2** Turn right up High Street.

■ **3** Turn left at the top of the hill at the junction with the A591. Proceed for 10m.

■ **4** Turn right. Cross the road to a large footpath sign to Orrest Head opposite. Turn left behind some metal railings. Turn right up a lane for 40m.

■ **5** Keep right at a footpath junction. Continue on the winding tarmac lane, climbing steadily through woodland. At Elleray Wood Cottage the lane ceases and becomes a broad stony path.

■ **6** Take the centre of three possible paths in a woodland clearing where there is a gate with ornamental wheels set into it to the right. The broad uphill path bends sharply right. Continue straight ahead at a wall corner on the right. Follow the terraced path passing bench-seats.

■ **7** Turn left at the end of the path. Go through a kissing-gate adjacent to a memorial stone with an inscribed verse by the poet Keble. Go ahead along a wall on the left. Ascend gradually,

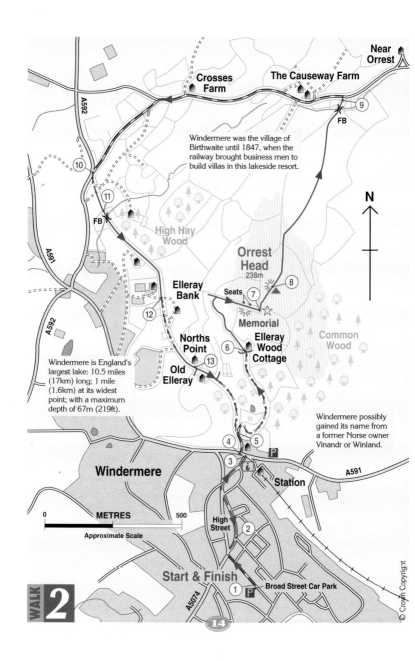

Crosses Farm

The Causeway Farm

Near Orrest

9
FB

Windermere was the village of Birthwaite until 1847, when the railway brought business men to build villas in this lakeside resort.

10

11
FB

High Hay Wood

Orrest Head
238m

N

Elleray Bank

Seats

7

8

Memorial

12

Norths Point

6

Elleray Wood Cottage

13

Old Elleray

Windermere is England's largest lake: 10.5 miles (17km) long; 1 mile (1.6km) at its widest point; with a maximum depth of 67m (219ft).

Common Wood

4
5

3

P

Windermere possibly gained its name from a former Norse owner Vinandr or Winland.

Windermere

A591

Station

0   METRES   500

Approximate Scale

High Street

2

Start & Finish

1
P
Broad Street Car Park

A5074

WALK 2

14

© Crown Copyright

Central Lakeland viewed across Windermere from Orrest Head

bending right to the broad summit of Orrest Head (238m/781ft).

■ **8** Turn left, descending a grassy path with walls coming in from left and right near the bottom. Cross a stile. The path veers right between hawthorn bushes, leaving the wall. Continue over broad grassland to the right of a telegraph post. On arriving at a wall with a wicket-gate, do not go through the gate. Continue along the wall on the left. Cross a stone footbridge. Proceed for 75m.

■ **9** Cross a stone-stepped stile adjacent to a field-gate onto a lane. Turn left. Follow the lane for 0.6 miles (1km). 150m after Crosses Farm on the right, fork left at a junction. The lane descends steeply whilst bending left to reach a junction with the A592.

■ **10** Do not go onto the A592, but turn sharp left at the junction and pass through ornamental wrought-iron gates

at a footpath sign to Orrest Head. Follow an uphill track over grassland, bending left up a slope. Leave the track after 100m at a ground-level footpath sign. Go ahead across a driveway.

■ **11** Pass through a wicket-gate into High Hay Wood. Cross a footbridge. Ascend a stony path. Pass two large houses on the right, later to cross a driveway to a house. Pass a kitchen garden to the right, after which the path narrows between high stone walls.

■ **12** Cut across the driveway to Elleray Bank House. Follow a narrow path opposite along a metal fence on the left.

■ **13** Pass between buildings of converted stables called Norths Point. Proceed on an ascending path with a high wall on the right. Keep straight ahead at a junction at the top of the rise. Turn right at (5) to retrace the outward route back to the car park.

WALK 3

AMBLESIDE - STOCK GHYLL - STOCKGHYLL FORCE - ROUNDHILL FARM
3 MILES (4.9 km)

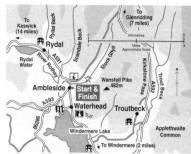

Route Details

Distance	3 miles (4.9 km)
Degree of Difficulty	Easy
Ascent	120m (394ft)
Time	2 hours

Start and Finish Points

Rydal Road car park, Ambleside (GR 376047).
From Keswick take the A591 south past Grasmere, and from Windermere the A591 north through Ambleside.
The car park is situated at the north end of Ambleside, off the A591, across a bridge, opposite an entrance to the Charlotte Mason College.

Maps Needed

OS Outdoor Leisure No 7 (1:25 000)
OS Landranger No 90 (1:50 000)

Parking Facilities

The large Rydal Road car park (GR 376047) at the north end of Ambleside has easy access to the facilities of the town. Should the car park be full, there are other car parks in the south, west and central areas of Ambleside.

Route Description

■ **1** Start by leaving the car park to the right of the toilets. Go over a footbridge onto the A591. Cross the road. Turn right to follow it into the centre of Ambleside.

■ **2** Go ahead where the road bends sharply right with the Salutation Hotel up on the left. Go along a narrow road between Barclays Bank on the left and the Market Hall on the right. Proceed for 25m. Turn left on an uphill narrow road with a variety of signs to the waterfalls/Stock Ghyll/Wansfell. Proceed for 350m.

■ **3** Fork left, off the road, through an unmarked wall gap adjacent to a field-gate. Follow a woodland path along Stock Ghyll on the left for 150m.

■ **4** Fork left down stone steps. Turn left over a footbridge. Immediately bear half-right up a wooded bankside. The path follows an iron safety fence on the right with the gill below.

■ **5** Fork right at the top of a rise. Follow a narrow path to the foot of Stockghyll Force. Return by the same route to (5). Turn right, up the stepped bankside to the top of the falls.

■ **6** Turn right to cross a stepped footbridge over the head of the falls.

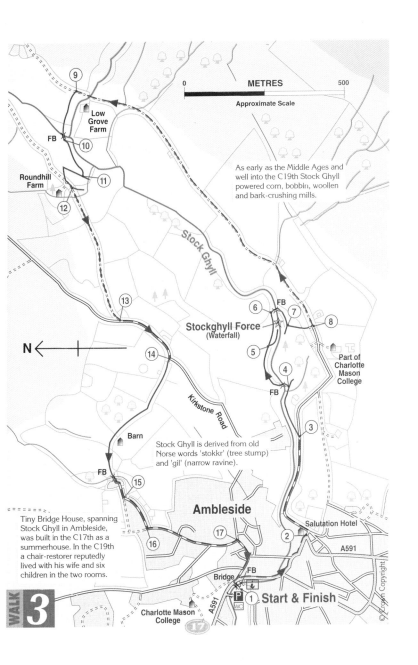

0   **METRES**   500

Approximate Scale

As early as the Middle Ages and well into the C19th Stock Ghyll powered corn, bobbin, woollen and bark-crushing mills.

⑨

Low Grove Farm

FB

⑩

Roundhill Farm

⑪

⑫

Stock Ghyll

⑬

⑥   FB   ⑦

Stockghyll Force
(Waterfall)

⑧

⑤

N ←

⑭

④

FB

Part of Charlotte Mason College

③

Kirkstone Road

Barn

Stock Ghyll is derived from old Norse words 'stokkr' (tree stump) and 'gil' (narrow ravine).

Ambleside

FB

⑮

Salutation Hotel

②

A591

Tiny Bridge House, spanning Stock Ghyll in Ambleside, was built in the C17th as a summerhouse. In the C19th a chair-restorer reputedly lived with his wife and six children in the two rooms.

⑯

⑰

Bridge

FB

P
WC

① **Start & Finish**

Charlotte Mason College

⑰

A591

© Crown Copyright

WALK 3

An early glimpse en route of Stockghyll Force

Immediately turn right along the iron fence on the right, descending over rocks.

■ **7** Take a left fork after 100m at a picnic-table. Go ahead through a turnstile iron gate. Proceed for 20m onto a tarmac lane.

■ **8** Turn left at a signpost to Kirkstone. Pass through a field-gate adjacent to a cattle-grid. Continue ahead on the lane to go through another field-gate adjacent to a cattle-grid.

■ **9** Turn left immediately after a third cattle-grid adjacent to a field-gate at a waymarked sign with Low Grove Farm on the left. Descend over grassland. Pass through a wicket-gate adjacent to a field-gate at the bottom of the slope. Straight ahead, cross over a broad footbridge spanning Stock Gyhll.

■ **10** Turn left on a grassy path along the gill on the left for 125m.

■ **11** Double back right, ascending the grassy bankside away from the gill. The path bends sharply left with Roundhill Farm up on the right.

■ **12** Go through a kissing-gate at the top of the bank. Bear left along a broad bridleway between walls.

■ **13** Turn left onto the narrow Kirkstone Road. Proceed downhill for 200m.

■ **14** Turn right where the road bends left at a footpath sign to Eller Rigg. Continue along a broad path between walls. Cross a stile adjacent to a field-gate at a barn on the left. Continue along a wall to the left. Pass through a gated wall gap at the field corner. Cross a stone slab footbridge. Go up steps through a metal-gated wall gap and down steps on the other side. The path bends right between cottages to emerge onto a lane.

■ **15** Fork left down the lane for 125m to a junction with a narrow road.

A sylvan pathway through Stockghyll Woods

■ **16** Turn left, downhill. After 100m join the Kirkstone Road.

■ **17** Turn right, downhill, along it. Cross the A591, entering the car park opposite over the bridge.

WALK 4

AMBLESIDE -
SCANDALE BECK -
HIGH SWEDEN BRIDGE -
LOW SWEDEN BRIDGE
3.4 MILES (5.4 km)

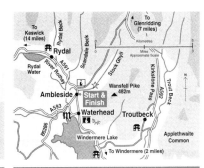

Route Details

Distance	3.4 miles (5.4 km)
Degree of Difficulty	Easy
Ascent	220m (722ft)
Time	2.5 hours

Start and Finish Points

Rydal Road car park, Ambleside (GR 376047).
From Keswick take the A591 south past Grasmere and from Windermere the A591 north through Ambleside.
The car park is situated at the north end of Ambleside, off the A591, across a bridge, opposite an entrance to the Charlotte Mason College.

Maps Needed

OS Outdoor Leisure No 7 (1:25 000)
OS Landranger No 90 (1:50 000)

Parking Facilities

The large Rydal Road car park (GR 376047) at the north end of Ambleside has easy access to the facilities of the town. Should the car park be full, there are other car parks in the south, west and central areas of Ambleside.

Route Description

■ **1** Start by leaving the car park entrance over the bridge. Cross the A591. Go up the Kirkstone Road opposite. After 50m pass a junction on the left. After a left bend in the road, proceed for 75m.

■ **2** Turn left up a 'no-through' narrow road signposted to High Sweden Bridge. Continue ahead, passing between houses.

■ **3** Pass through a field-gate. Go ahead on a broad ascending path with Scandale Beck below on the left. Note the distant views of Rydal Water over the wall on the left.

■ **4** Go through a field-gate, entering a wood.

■ **5** Pass through another field-gate to emerge from the wood. Proceed for 150m.

■ **6** Fork left, leaving the main path, down a narrow path to High Sweden Bridge, a narrow packhorse bridge spanning Scandale Beck. Turn left, over the bridge.

■ **7** Immediately turn right. Pass through a wicket-gate. Immediately turn left up a narrow path along a low broken wall on the right. Ahead, pass over a very high ladder-stile.

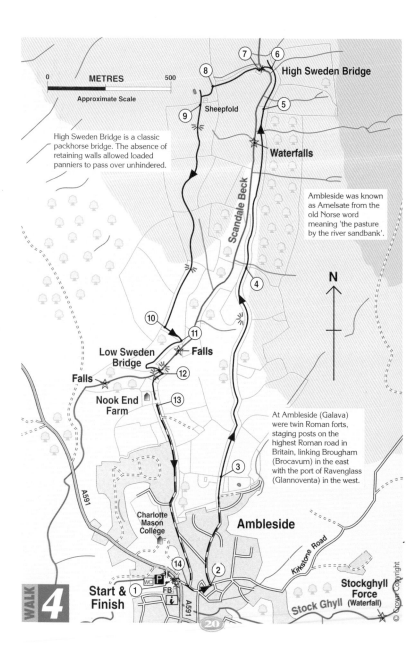

0   METRES   500
Approximate Scale

High Sweden Bridge is a classic packhorse bridge. The absence of retaining walls allowed loaded panniers to pass over unhindered.

High Sweden Bridge

Sheepfold

Waterfalls

Scandale Beck

Ambleside was known as Amelsate from the old Norse word meaning 'the pasture by the river sandbank'.

N

Low Sweden Bridge

Falls

Falls

Nook End Farm

At Ambleside (Galava) were twin Roman forts, staging posts on the highest Roman road in Britain, linking Brougham (Brocavum) in the east with the port of Ravenglass (Glannoventa) in the west.

Charlotte Mason College

Ambleside

A591

Kirkstone Road

WALK 4

Start & Finish

Stockghyll Force (Waterfall)

Stock Ghyll

20

© Crown Copyright

■ **8** Bear diagonally left over rolling grassland, bending right towards a wall. Bear right with the wall on the left. Turn left crossing the lower of two ladder-stiles to the right of a double sheepfold.

■ **9** Proceed ahead down the grassy fellside on a broad path, en route passing over three ladder-stiles adjacent to field-gates. Ahead are distant aerial views over Ambleside and Windermere to the fells beyond.

■ **10** Turn sharp left along a wall on the right.

■ **11** Turn right through a field-gate at a wall corner. The broad path bends left downhill with Scandale Beck below on the left. Go over Low Sweden Bridge across Scandale Beck. Note the waterfalls up on the left and below on the right.

■ **12** Immediately turn right with the beck now on the right. Continue up the broad path. Pass through a field-gate. Go through another field-gate entering the yard of Nook End Farm. Pass through the yard with the farm on the right.

■ **13** Emerge onto a lane through a kissing-gate adjacent to a field-gate. Continue downhill, passing first a library building on the right and then behind Charlotte Mason College, also on the right.

■ **14** Turn right, downhill, at the junction with the Kirkstone Road. Cross the A591. Enter the car park opposite, over the bridge.

Ancient High Sweden Bridge, spanning tumbling Scandale Beck

WALK 5

NEAR SAWREY - DUB HOW FARM - FAR SAWREY - WILFIN BECK

3.1 MILES (5 km)

Route Details

Distance	3.1 miles (5 km)
Degree of Difficulty	Easy
Ascent	120m (394ft)
Time	2 hours

Start and Finish Points

Lay-by with a telephone kiosk (GR 339958) at Near Sawrey on the B5285 Hawkshead to Bowness Ferry road, opposite Beech Mount Country House Hotel.

Maps Needed

OS Outdoor Leisure No 7 (1:25 000)
OS Landranger No 96 (1:50 000)

Parking Facilities

As the lay-by parking (GR 339958) is limited, there may be some parking spaces in the village of Near Sawrey. To visit Hill Top, the former home of Beatrix Potter, turn left from the lay-by, along the B5285, turning right after 300m. Hill Top is a National Trust property which is open to the public. The car park is only for visitors of the house, and is not to be used by walkers.

Route Description

■ **1** Start by turning right on the road. Proceed for 40m.

■ **2** Turn left. Cross the road. Go down the minor road opposite. Pass through the picturesque village of Near Sawrey.

■ **3** Fork right at the end of the village onto another minor road. Proceed for 300m.

■ **4** Fork left at a junction onto a narrow, leafy lane with Esthwaite over to the right. Proceed for 900m, passing Out Dubs Tarn away down to the right and Dub How Farm on the left.

■ **5** Turn left at a footpath sign to Far Sawrey. Cross a stile over a fence. Go through a narrow enclosure and over another fence stile. Go straight ahead up a path through woodland for 75m.

■ **6** Fork right onto an uphill woodland footpath marked by a yellow waymarker, bending left with a wire fence to the right.

■ **7** Emerge from the wood over a stile in a wire fence. Enter broad grassland between wooded areas. Go straight ahead to pass over a stile adjacent to a field-gate.

■ **8** Ahead, pass through another field-gate. Continue on a rutted track through meadowland for 100m.

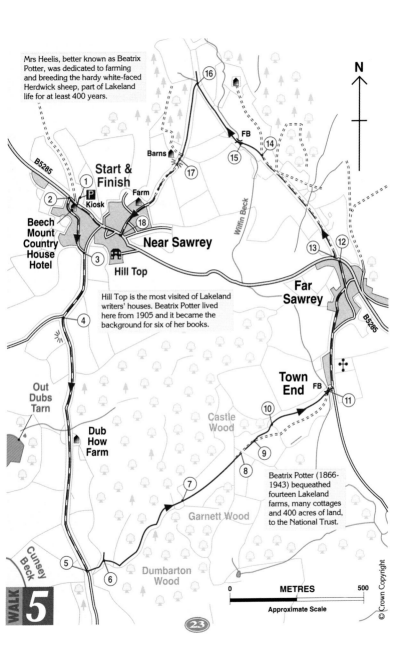

Mrs Heelis, better known as Beatrix Potter, was dedicated to farming and breeding the hardy white-faced Herdwick sheep, part of Lakeland life for at least 400 years.

N

B5285

Start & Finish

Barns

1

2
Kiosk

Farm

Beech Mount Country House Hotel

18

Near Sawrey

3

Hill Top

Hill Top is the most visited of Lakeland writers' houses. Beatrix Potter lived here from 1905 and it became the background for six of her books.

4

Out Dubs Tarn

Dub How Farm

Castle Wood

7

Garnett Wood

Cunsey Beck

5

6

Dumbarton Wood

FB

16

17

15

14

Willin Beck

13

12

Far Sawrey

B5285

Town End

FB

11

10

9

8

Beatrix Potter (1866-1943) bequeathed fourteen Lakeland farms, many cottages and 400 acres of land, to the National Trust.

METRES

0   500

Approximate Scale

© Crown Copyright

WALK
5

23

The nearby Ferry House on the western shore of beautiful Windermere

■ **9** Fork left onto a terraced path, leaving the track. The path passes along a wire fence enclosing a copse on the left. Bend left to cross a stile adjacent to a field-gate.

■ **10** Continue along a wall on the left. Cross a footbridge approaching the end of the path.

■ **11** Pass through a kissing-gate, adjacent to a field-gate, onto a minor road. Turn left, passing cottages on the left at Town End and a church on the hill on the right. Pass through the village of Far Sawrey. Bear left at a fork towards the end of the village.

■ **12** Emerge onto the B5285. Cross it. Turn left for 10m.

■ **13** Turn right up a lane. Pass through a kissing-gate adjacent to a cattle-grid and a field-gate after 400m. Proceed for a further 100m.

■ **14** Fork left at a signpost to Hawkshead, leaving what has become a driveway to a house. Proceed along a broad bridlepath with Wilfin Beck on the left.

■ **15** Pass over a footbridge. Continue ahead, passing over a stile adjacent to a field-gate. Pass over another stile adjacent to a field-gate at a footpath junction.

■ **16** Double back left, following a signpost to Near Sawrey on a broad bridlepath between walls. Pass over a stile adjacent to a field-gate with barns on the right.

■ **17** Continue ahead, passing through a farm-gate with a farm on the right. Now on a narrow road, go through the village of Near Sawrey to the junction with the B5285.

■ **18** Turn right on the road. Proceed for 200m to the parking lay-by on the right.

WALK 6

BLELHAM TARN - OUTGATE - WINDERMERE LAKE - WRAY CASTLE -
4.4 MILES (7 km)

Distance	4.4 miles (7 km)
Degree of Difficulty	Easy
Ascent	90m (295ft)
Time	3 hours

Start and Finish Points

Wray Castle car park (GR 375010), just past the house at the end of a driveway. The car park is situated off a minor road, between Low Wray Bridge and the hamlet of High Wray, south of Ambleside and north-east of Hawkshead.

Maps Needed

OS Outdoor Leisure No 7 (1:25 000)
OS Landranger No 90 (1:50 000)
OS Landranger No 96 (1:50 000)

Parking Facilities

There is limited parking on the low car park west of Wray Castle by kind permission of the National Trust. Please do not park in front of the Castle. Wray Castle is not open to the public, but occasionally its tea room is. This is the only feasible parking area on the route of the walk.

Route Description

■ **1** From the car park return along Wray Castle driveway. Pass through the entrance gates.

■ **2** Turn right, down the road, bending left over Low Wray Bridge. Continue ahead for 200m.

■ **3** Turn left through a field-gate at a footpath sign to Outgate. Fork left after 75m at a ground-level sign to Outgate. Follow a broad path across grassland with Blelham Tarn over on the left.

■ **4** Pass through a kissing-gate into woodland. Cross a stile. Proceed ahead past the head of the tarn on the left. Pass over a stile. Continue along the edge of Spicka Coppice to emerge through a field-gate. Continue for 100m.

■ **5** Filter left onto the narrow B5286. Proceed towards the hamlet of Outgate for 150m.

■ **6** Turn left at a footpath sign. Follow a lane between cottages to pass through a wicket-gate. Go ahead descending over meadowland. Pass to the right of a telegraph pole.

■ **7** Cross a footbridge. Immediately pass over a stile. Bear right, uphill, over grassland to the wall on the right. Pass over a high ladder-stile to the left. Continue ahead over a hummock.

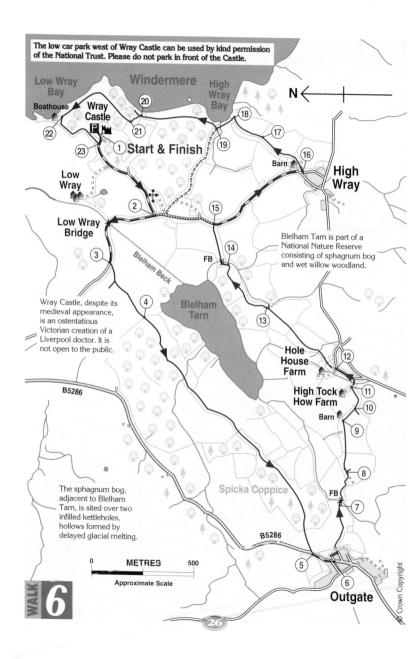

The low car park west of Wray Castle can be used by kind permission of the National Trust. Please do not park in front of the Castle.

N ←

Low Wray Bay

Windermere

High Wray Bay

Boathouse

Wray Castle

20

18

22

21

Start & Finish

19

17

23

1

16

Barn

Low Wray

High Wray

2

15

Low Wray Bridge

Blelham Beck

FB

14

Blelham Tarn is part of a National Nature Reserve consisting of sphagnum bog and wet willow woodland.

3

Blelham Tarn

4

13

Hole House Farm

12

Wray Castle, despite its medieval appearance, is an ostentatious Victorian creation of a Liverpool doctor. It is not open to the public.

High Tock How Farm

11

10

B5286

Barn

9

8

Spicka Coppice

FB

7

The sphagnum bog, adjacent to Blelham Tarn, is sited over two infilled kettleholes, hollows formed by delayed glacial melting.

0   METRES   500

Approximate Scale

B5286

5

6

WALK

6

26

Outgate

© Crown Copyright

■ **8** Bear left 15m after the telegraph pole on the left. Follow an uphill path to pass through a field-gate. Continue ahead uphill.

■ **9** Turn right along a wall on the left at three field-gates with a barn on the left. Proceed for 100m.

■ **10** Go through a field-gate at a footpath junction. The grassy path bends left, downhill, with High Tock How Farm away to the left. Pass over a stile at the bottom of the slope.

■ **11** Turn right on the farm driveway which filters left onto a minor road. Proceed for 100m.

Peace reigns over tranquil Blelham Tarn

■ **12** Go straight ahead where the road bends right at a low-level footpath sign. Pass through the yard of Hole House Farm. Emerge from the yard over a stone-stepped stile. Go ahead on a path which passes over grassland with Blelham Tarn below on the left. Pass over a stile. Continue ahead on the winding downhill path.

■ **13** Pass over a stile at the bottom of the slope. Cross a field along a wire-fence on the right. Pass over another stile. Pass along the edge of another field. Follow waymarked signs. The path bends right to pass through trees.

■ **14** Emerge from the trees through a kissing-gate. Immediately cross a stone slab footbridge. Follow the waymarking ahead. Pass through a field-gate onto the road.

■ **15** Turn right along the road uphill into the hamlet of High Wray.

■ **16** Turn left where the road bends right at a bridleway sign to the lake. Pass through a wicket-gate. Proceed for 15m. Turn left over a stone-stepped stile at the corner of a high barn. Follow a field-path along a high wall on the left. Pass through a kissing-gate into another field. Descend towards Windermere lakeshore.

■ **17** Pass between gateposts at the field bottom. Continue through the next field along a wall on the left. Cross over a stile.

■ **18** Immediately turn left at a bridleway sign for Wray Church. Pass through a stepped wall gap. Follow the path round High Wray Bay. Go through a wicket-gate. Follow the bridleway to High Wray Church. Proceed for 50m.

■ **19** Turn right over a stile and continue round the lakeshore on the right.

■ **20** Turn left at a wood with a shingled beach on the right. Follow up a path with the wood on the right.

■ **21** Turn right over a stile adjacent to a gate at the top of the slope. Proceed on a woodland path towards the large castellated boathouse.

■ **22** Turn left before the boathouse. Go up a narrow path skirting the wood. Go up steps into the forecourt of Wray Castle.

■ **23** Bear left across the forecourt and down into the car park.

WALK 7

WHITE MOSS COMMON - RYDAL MOUNT - RYDAL WATER - RYDAL CAVE
4.6 MILES (7.5 km)

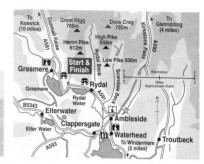

Route Details

Distance	4.6 miles (7.5 km)
Degree of Difficulty	Moderate
Ascent	210m (689ft)
Time	3.5 hours

Start and Finish Points

White Moss Common National Trust pay and display car park (GR 349066), off the A591, is situated on the left 1.5 miles (2.4km) south-east of Grasmere, and on the right 2.2 miles (3.5km) north-west of Ambleside through Rydal village.

Maps Needed

OS Outdoor Leisure No 7 (1:25 000)
OS Landranger No 90 (1:50 000)

Parking Facilities

There is another car park (GR 350065) 150m west of the start and finish points on the opposite side of the A591, close to the northern shore of Rydal Water and the banks of the River Rothay. Both car parks are large and very popular during the summer months. Toilets and picnic facilities are available.

Route Description

■ **1** Start from the higher car park (GR 349066). Turn left when facing the National Trust notice board at the entrance. Go up the minor road, off the A591, leading away from the car park. Continue for 700m.

■ **2** Turn right through a wicket-gate adjacent to a field-gate 16m after a small garage on the right. Turn left up a woodland loop path with a wall and the road on the left. Continue downhill to go through an iron gate in a wall. Emerge from woodland to filter right back onto the road. Continue ahead.

■ **3** Turn right at a road junction with How Top Farm on the left. Go up a minor 'no-through' road signposted to Rydal/Alcock Tarn. Bend left and right, uphill. Proceed ahead on the level road.

■ **4** Turn sharp right with tiny White Moss Tarn on the left and two cottages beyond it. Cross a footbridge. Go up a narrow path to the summit of White Moss Common (142m/466ft). Return to (4). Turn right to continue along the narrow walled lane.

■ **5** Continue ahead with a plantation on the left. Pass through a wicket-gate. Go ahead on a walled path to pass

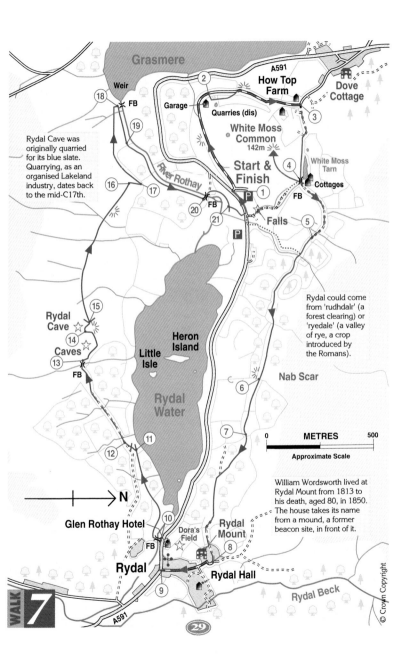

Grasmere

A591

How Top Farm

Dove Cottage

Weir

18 FB

Garage

Quarries (dis)

2

3

19

White Moss Common
142m

White Moss Tarn

4

Cottages

Rydal Cave was originally quarried for its blue slate. Quarrying, as an organised Lakeland industry, dates back to the mid-C17th.

River Rothay

16

17

Start & Finish

P

1

20

FB

21

P

FB

Falls

5

Rydal could come from 'rudhdalr' (a forest clearing) or 'ryedales' (a valley of rye, a crop introduced by the Romans).

15

Rydal Cave ☆

Heron Island

14 ☆

Caves

13

FB

Little Isle

Rydal Water

Nab Scar

6

7

METRES   0   500

Approximate Scale

11

12

→ N

Glen Rothay Hotel

FB

10

Dora's Field ☆

Rydal Mount

8

Rydal

9

Rydal Hall

William Wordsworth lived at Rydal Mount from 1813 to his death, aged 80, in 1850. The house takes its name from a mound, a former beacon site, in front of it.

A591

Rydal Beck

WALK 7

29

© Crown Copyright

through another wicket-gate. Continue ahead on a woodland path. Go through a field-gate to emerge from the wood.

■ **6** Proceed ahead on a terraced path along a wall on the left and sloping grassland to the right. Pass through a wall gap.

■ **7** Go through a field-gate. The broad path bears right down the fell, then bends left uphill. Pass through a field-gate. Follow the walled path to go through another field-gate. Proceed for 40m, passing behind the white house of Rydal Mount.

■ **8** Turn right, down a minor road, with Rydal Mount and gardens on the right. Towards the bottom of the road, pass the entrance to the Church of St Mary and Dora's Field on the right in Rydal village.

■ **9** Cross the A591. Turn right along the road. Proceed for 130m as far as the Glen Rothay Hotel on the right.

■ **10** Turn left, off the road, at a footpath sign. Descend to cross a footbridge over the River Rothay. Bear right with the river on the right. Pass through a kissing-gate into woodland. Pass through another kissing-gate to emerge from the wood with Rydal Water shore on the right.

■ **11** Immediately fork left, up the bankside, away from the lake. Pass over diagonal cross-paths.

■ **12** Filter right at the top of the rise onto a broad, gradually ascending path. Cross a stone bridge as the path bends left uphill.

■ **13** Bend right, along a wall on the right, passing caves of a former slate quarry on the left. Bend left, uphill, to arrive at Rydal Cave. This spacious interior contains a small shallow tarn.

■ **14** Turn right at the cave.

Proceed for 130m.

■ **15** Follow the middle of three paths. Continue along the terraced path contouring the fellside. Ignore branch paths, keeping on the higher level.

■ **16** Turn right down the ridge of a grassy shoulder. Proceed 100m to a col.

Rydal Water, beloved by William Wordsworth

■ **17** Bear left, downhill, along a wall on the right with the fell sloping uphill on the left. Proceed for 400m. Bear right down steps to a footbridge.

■ **18** Do not cross the footbridge. Turn right along the River Rothay on the left.

■ **19** Pass through a kissing-gate. Continue through woodland with the river on the left. Go through a kissing-gate. Proceed for 300m.

■ **20** Turn left over a footbridge. Bear right on a broad path, bending right and ascending gradually.

■ **21** After 100 metres, fork left to go up some steps. Bear right, then left to the A591. Cross the road. Return to the car park.

WALK 8

GRASMERE - DOVE COTTAGE - ALCOCK TARN - GREENHEAD GILL

3 MILES (4.9 km)

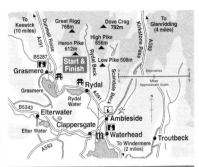

Route Details

Distance	3 miles (4.9 km)
Degree of Difficulty	Moderate/Strenuous
Ascent	285m (935ft)
Time	3 hours

Start and Finish Points

Stock Lane car park (GR 339073) off the B5287 into Grasmere.
From Keswick follow the A591 south towards Ambleside. Ignore the right turn into Grasmere opposite the Swan Hotel. Take the next right turn onto the B5287 towards Grasmere.
From Ambleside take the A591 north, turning left onto the B5287 at the first junction into Grasmere.

Maps Needed

OS Outdoor Leisure No 7 (1:25 000)
OS Landranger No 90 (1:50 000)

Parking Facilities

Apart from the Stock Lane car park (GR 339073) there are two other large pay and display car parks in Grasmere: Red Bank Road (GR 337074) and Broadgate Meadows (GR 338077).

Route Description

■ **1** Start by leaving the entrance to the car park. Turn left onto Stock Lane. Continue ahead.

■ **2** Cross diagonally right over the A591 Keswick/Windermere road at crossroads. Take the minor road left to Dove Cottage. Continue ahead for 250m.

■ **3** Bear left at a road junction with How Top Farm on the right. Go up a 'no-through' road, following a footpath sign to Alcock Tarn and Rydal. Proceed uphill for 150m.

■ **4** Turn left, off the road, at a bench-seat where the road bends right. Follow a sign to Alcock Tarn on a walled path, entering woodland.

■ **5** Take the left fork, downhill, through a field-gate, ignoring the steep uphill fork to the right. The uphill path passes through a field-gate to emerge from woodland. Continue climbing gradually, bending right, then zig-zagging. Pass an artificial tarn on the right.

■ **6** Pass through a wicket-gate with a sign to Alcock Tarn. Continue uphill with a wall up on the right. Bending left, cross a gill over a footbridge. The path climbs, bending right to the summit of Grey Crag (350m/1148ft).

■ **7** Leave the summit half-left on a

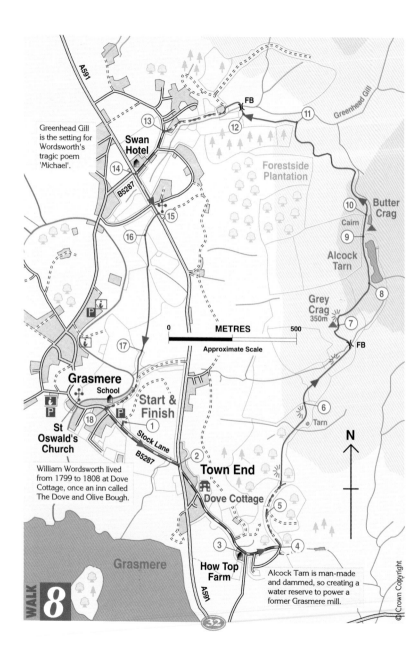

Greenhead Gill is the setting for Wordsworth's tragic poem 'Michael'.

Swan Hotel

Forestside Plantation

Butter Crag

Cairn

Alcock Tarn

Grey Crag 350m

FB

METRES

0   500

Approximate Scale

Grasmere

School

Start & Finish

St Oswald's Church

Tarn

N

William Wordsworth lived from 1799 to 1808 at Dove Cottage, once an inn called The Dove and Olive Bough.

Town End

Dove Cottage

Grasmere

How Top Farm

Alcock Tarn is man-made and dammed, so creating a water reserve to power a former Grasmere mill.

WALK 8

© Crown Copyright

Grasmere village and its lake couched beneath Helm Crag and distant Steel Fell

path which leads through a gap in a wall. Proceed on the broad grassy track, veering left to Alcock Tarn.

■ **8** Turn left and follow the western shore of the tarn.

■ **9** Pass over a stile adjacent to a gate in a wall at the north-west corner of the tarn. Continue along a wall on the left. Pass a large cairn, with Butter Crag away up on the right.

■ **10** Bear left at a wall corner on the left. The broad twisting path descends diagonally left over grassland to the corner of a plantation. Continue diagonally downhill to another corner of the plantation.

■ **11** Turn left at the wall corner. Follow along Greenhead Gill on the right.

■ **12** Turn right across a footbridge. Turn immediately left and pass through a field-gate. Continue ahead, downhill, on a tarmac footpath with the gill on the left.

■ **13** Turn left at the junction onto a narrow road which bends right, downhill. Arrive at the Swan Hotel on the right, at the side of the A591.

■ **14** Turn left along the A591 on the right. Continue ahead, crossing over a road junction.

■ **15** Turn right to cross the road, just after the church on the left. Pass through the field-gate opposite at a footpath sign. Continue ahead on a broad, grassy path which bends left to pass through a field-gate.

■ **16** Proceed straight across three fields using three kissing-gates adjacent to field-gates.

■ **17** On emerging from the last field, pass through a small enclosure with the River Rothay to the right. Go through a kissing-gate adjacent to a field-gate. Follow a tarmac path. Pass through a school playground.

■ **18** Turn left onto Stock Lane. Follow the road to return to the car park on the left.

WALK 9

GRASMERE - FAR EASEDALE GILL - EASEDALE TARN - SOURMILK GILL -

5 MILES (8 km)

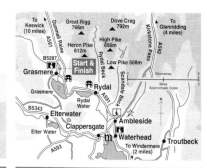

Route Details

Distance	5 miles (8 km)
Degree of Difficulty	Moderate
Ascent	235m (771ft)
Time	3.5 hours

Start and Finish Points

Broadgate Meadow car park (GR 338077) on the left, off the B5287 into Grasmere village.
From Keswick follow the A591 south towards Ambleside. Turn right on the B5287 into Grasmere.
From Ambleside take the A591 north, ignoring the first turn left into Grasmere and taking the next left turn onto the B5287, with the Swan Hotel on the right.

Maps Needed

OS Outdoor Leisure No 7 (1:25 000)
OS Landranger No 90 (1:50 000)

Parking Facilities

Apart from the Broadgate Meadow car park (GR 338077), there are two other large car parks in Grasmere: Stock Lane (GR 339073) and Red Bank Road (GR 337074).

Route Description

■ **1** Start from the car park entrance. Cross over the B5287. Turn right along the road. Proceed for 300m.
■ **2** Turn left just before the road bridge. Go through a kissing-gate adjacent to a field-gate at a footpath sign. The path bends left, uphill, through trees with the River Rothay below on the right. Pass through a field-gate at the end of the path.
■ **3** Turn right along the Easedale Road. Pass a small car park on the right. Follow the road until it bends right. Do not follow the signpost to Easedale Tarn.
■ **4** Bear right through the gateway to Lancrigg Guest House, leaving the road. Follow a permissive footpath up a lane. Pass over cross-paths before going through a wicket-gate adjacent to a cattle-grid. Continue up the driveway.
■ **5** Fork right at the entrance to Lancrigg Guest House on a path which bends left behind the house. Go between farm buildings. Continue ahead to pass through a wicket-gate and enter Lancrigg Wood. Proceed to the Wordsworth memorial stone on the right.
■ **6** Continue ahead. Bear left at a waymarked fork to skirt a former pond

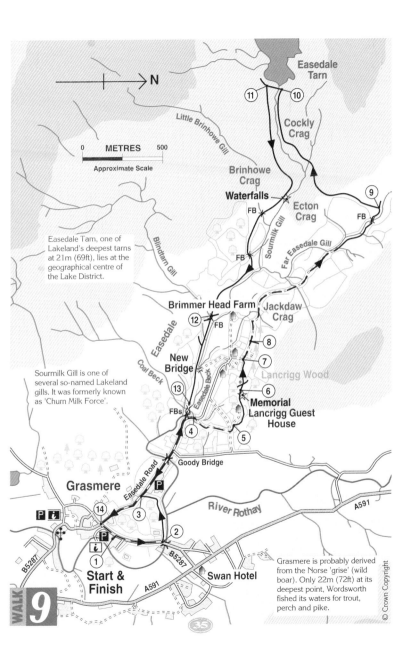

N

0 METRES 500
Approximate Scale

Easedale Tarn

Little Brinhowe Gill

Cockly Crag

Brinhowe Crag

Waterfalls

Ecton Crag

FB

Easedale Tarn, one of Lakeland's deepest tarns at 21m (69ft), lies at the geographical centre of the Lake District.

Blindtarn Gill

Sourmilk Gill

Far Easedale Gill

FB

FB

Brimmer Head Farm

Jackdaw Crag

Easedale

Coal Beck

New Bridge

Lancrigg Wood

Easedale Beck

Sourmilk Gill is one of several so-named Lakeland gills. It was formerly known as 'Churn Milk Force'.

Memorial Lancrigg Guest House

FBs

Goody Bridge

Grasmere

Easedale Road

River Rothay

A591

P

P

P

Start & Finish

Swan Hotel

A591

B5287

B5287

Grasmere is probably derived from the Norse 'grise' (wild boar). Only 22m (72ft) at its deepest point, Wordsworth fished its waters for trout, perch and pike.

© Crown Copyright

WALK 9

on the left. Pass through a wall gap and down steps. Emerge from the wood through a kissing-gate. Descend steps onto a stony lane.

Looking down Sourmilk Gill over to Helm Crag

■ **7** Turn right through a field-gate. Go along a wall on the left. Proceed for 60m.

■ **8** Go ahead on a broad downhill path signposted Far Easedale and Borrowdale at a wall corner. The broad stony walled path ascends gradually, joining Far Easedale Gill on the left. Cross a footbridge with a rock as its central buttress. Go ahead for 150m on a rising path.

■ **9** Take a left fork leaving the main path to follow a path up the fellside with a wall away to the left. Gradually it levels out, contouring right round the lower hillside on the right. It bends right and ascends along Sourmilk Gill on the left.

■ **10** Turn left at the foot of Easedale Tarn. Ford the shallow outlet stream, Sourmilk Gill. (If unfordable after heavy rain, return by outward route). Go ahead uphill for 60m.

■ **11** Turn left on a broad downhill bridlepath with Sourmilk Gill now on the

left. It bends right, passing the waterfalls on the left. Cross a footbridge. Pass between walls over a stone slab footbridge. Go through a kissing-gate at the bottom of the slope. Continue ahead through a field-gate. The path bends right over grassland with Brimmer Head Farm away to the left.

■ **12** Cross a concrete footbridge over a rivulet at cross-paths. Pass through the left of two adjacent metal field-gates at a wall sign on the left to Grasmere. Go ahead along the beck on the left with a wall on the right, passing New Bridge on the left to emerge onto open grassland.

■ **13** Pass through a field-gate. Continue ahead to pass through trees over a stone slab footbridge. Cross a stepped footbridge to emerge at (4) onto Easedale Road. Turn right along the road. Follow the outward route, to (3). Continue ahead to the junction with the B5287 in Grasmere village.

■ **14** Turn left along the B5287 on the right. Proceed for 150m. Turn right to cross the road. Enter the car park.

Tarn Crag looming large above Easedale Tarn

WALK 10

GRASMERE - GREENBURN VALLEY - GIBSON KNOTT - HELM CRAG

7.5 MILES (12 km)

Route Details

Distance	7.5 miles (12 km)
Degree of Difficulty	Strenuous
Ascent	370m (1213ft)
Time	5 hours

Start and Finish Points

Broadgate Meadow car park (GR 338077) on the left, off the B5287, into Grasmere village.
From Keswick follow the A591 south towards Ambleside, turning right on the B5287 into Grasmere.
From Ambleside take the A591 north, ignoring the first turn left into Grasmere and taking the next left turn onto the B5287, with the Swan Hotel on the right.

Maps Needed

OS Outdoor Leisure No 7 (1:25 000)
OS Landranger No 90 (1:50 000)

Parking Facilities

Apart from the Broadgate Meadow car park (GR 338077), there are two other large pay and display car parks in Grasmere: Stock Lane (GR 339073) and Red Bank Road (GR 337074).

Route Description

■ **1** Start from the car park entrance. Cross over the B5287. Turn right along the road for 300m.

■ **2** Turn left just before the road bridge through a kissing-gate adjacent to a field-gate at a footpath sign. Follow an uphill path through woodland with the River Rothay below on the right. Pass through a field-gate at the end of the path.

■ **3** Turn right along the Easedale Road. Pass a small pay and display car park on the right. Proceed to cross Goody Bridge. Continue on the road for another 65m.

■ **4** Turn right onto a lane. Follow it for 0.7 miles (1.1km) to fork left at a junction at Low Mill Bridge over to the right. Pass a farm on the left at Gyhll Foot. Go over a humpback bridge.

■ **5** Immediately take the left fork uphill on a driveway, leaving the road. Pass through two successive gates adjacent to cattle-grids. Bend left, passing two cottages on the right. Pass through the field-gate ahead onto grassland with a sign indicating Green Burn. Proceed for 16m.

■ **6** Bear right on a downhill path along a wall on the left. Go through a field-

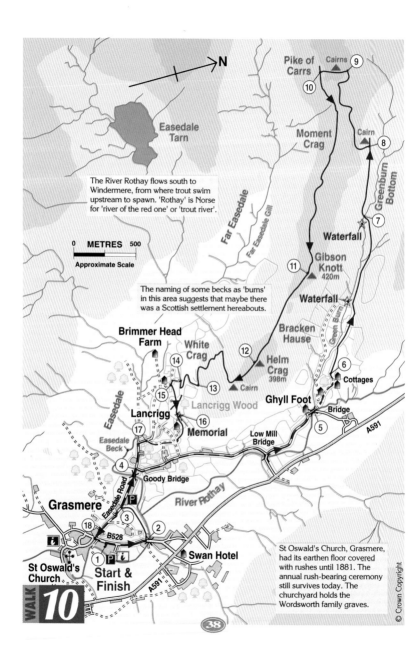

→N

Pike of Carrs Cairns ⑨

⑩

Moment Crag

Cairn ⑧

Greenburn Bottom

Easedale Tarn

The River Rothay flows south to Windermere, from where trout swim upstream to spawn. 'Rothay' is Norse for 'river of the red one' or 'trout river'.

⑦

Waterfall

0   METRES   500
Approximate Scale

Far Easedale

Far Easedale Gill

Gibson Knott 420m

⑪

The naming of some becks as 'burns' in this area suggests that maybe there was a Scottish settlement hereabouts.

Waterfall

Green Burn

Bracken Hause

Brimmer Head Farm

White Crag

⑫

Helm Crag 398m

⑥

Cottages

⑭

⑮

Cairn ⑬

Lancrigg Wood

Ghyll Foot

Bridge

A591

Lancrigg

⑯ Memorial

Low Mill Bridge

⑤

⑰

Easedale Beck

Easedale

④

Goody Bridge

Easedale Road

River Rothay

Grasmere

P

③

②

⑱

B528

P

Swan Hotel

St Oswald's Church

Start & Finish

A591

St Oswald's Church, Grasmere, had its earthen floor covered with rushes until 1881. The annual rush-bearing ceremony still survives today. The churchyard holds the Wordsworth family graves.

WALK 10

38

© Crown Copyright

gate. Continue with a wall on the right and Green Burn below on the left. Keep ahead to go through another field-gate. Pass a waterfall away to the left. Pass a second waterfall. Bend left round a grassy knoll.

■ **7** Ford shallow Green Burn. Immediately turn right, uphill, along the burn on the right.

■ **8** Turn left (SW) at a cairned junction on the top of a rise with a large cracked boulder 70m ahead. Ascend the fellside, bending left (S) on a faint path with some small cairns. Bend round right (W), climbing gradually.

■ **9** Bend sharp left (SSW) on a shelf, following some cairns. Proceed for 150m.

■ **10** Turn left (ESE) at a junction with the undulating ridge path, following it to the summit cairn of Gibson Knott (420m/1378ft).

■ **11** Continue ahead (SE) from the summit, descending to cross the grassy saddle of Bracken Hause. The path now zig-zags, finally bending left onto the craggy north-west summit of Helm Crag (398m/1305ft).

■ **12** Continue along the summit ridge (SE) to another rocky outcrop on the left. Descend quite steeply ahead (S) towards Grasmere below. Curve right (SE) round a grassy saddle at a low cairn. Descend a shaly track, bending left.

■ **13** Turn right at a wall corner on the right. Follow a stepped path, downhill, along the wall on the left. Bend right near the bottom along a wooden fence on the left. Bend left, passing a small disused quarry on the left. Bend right again to join a wall on the left. Proceed for 50m.

■ **14** Turn left down an unmarked stony lane between walls. Turn left after 100m at a footpath sign to Grasmere.

Turn right through a field-gate after 60m.

■ **15** Immediately turn left up steps with a sign indicating a permissive footpath through Lancrigg Wood via Wordsworth Memorial. Pass through a kissing-gate into woodland. Go up stone steps and through a wall gap. The path bends round a former pond on the right to take a waymarked fork.

Helm Crag viewed across Easedale Beck

■ **16** Go straight on from the Wordsworth Memorial Stone. Pass through a wicket-gate. Go ahead to bend right and left between farm buildings. Bend right behind Lancrigg House to filter left onto a lane. Go through a wicket-gate adjacent to a cattle-grid. Pass over cross-paths. Filter left between gate pillars onto Easedale Road at the foot of the lane.

■ **17** Go along the road, passing (4) and (3), to the junction with the B5287 in Grasmere village.

■ **18** Turn left. Proceed for 150m. Turn right to cross the road and enter the car park.

ELTERWATER - COLWITH FORCE - SKELWITH FORCE - ELTER WATER

5 MILES (8 km)

Route Details

Distance	5 miles (8 km)
Degree of Difficulty	Easy/Moderate
Ascent	160m (525ft)
Time	3.5 hours

Start and Finish Points

Car park (GR 328047) in Elterwater village immediately before the road bridge. Leave Ambleside south-west on the A593 Coniston road. On entering Skelwith Bridge bear right at a junction onto the B5343 Langdale road. After 1.4 miles (2.3 km) turn left on a minor road into Elterwater. From Coniston take the A593 Ambleside road north. After 3.7 miles (6km) turn left onto a minor road into Elterwater. The car park is on the right after crossing the road bridge

Maps Needed

OS Outdoor Leisure No 7 (1:25 000)
OS Landranger No 90 (1:50 000)

Parking Facilities

If the car park (GR 328047) is full, there is limited parking north of the village, off the B5343.

Route Description

■ **1** Start by leaving the car park entrance. Turn left on the road. Cross the road bridge over Great Langdale Beck. Proceed for 220m.

■ **2** Take the right fork up a lane with the Eltermere Country House Hotel on the left.

■ **3** Follow up a broad path marked 'unsuitable for motors'. Pass through a field-gate at the top of a rise. Continue ahead.

■ **4** Turn left at a footpath sign. Go through a kissing-gate. Cross over grassland. Descend to pass through a wall gap. Continue on a field path. Go over a stile into the next field.

■ **5** Continue ahead through a gate into the yard of Wilson Place Farm. Leave the farmyard through a gate. Go down a short driveway to the road.

■ **6** Turn left on the road. Proceed for 70m.

■ **7** Turn right through a kissing-gate. Descend the grassy slope ahead. Go up steps at the bottom. Cross a footbridge over Greenburn Beck. Go through a wicket-gate. Descend steps.

■ **8** Bend right, then left on an uphill path towards a wall corner. Cross over a stile. Climb a narrow path. Pass to the

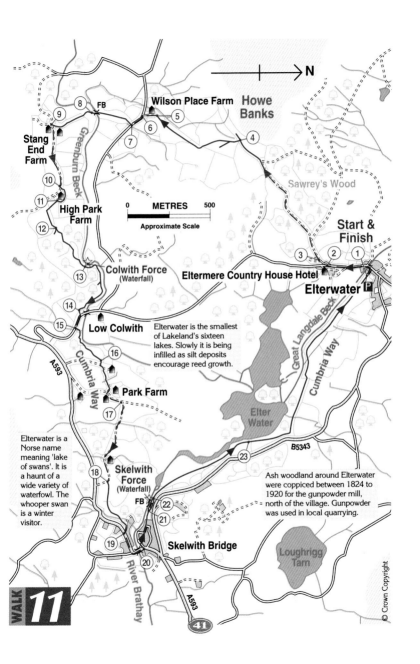

→ N

Wilson Place Farm

Howe Banks

FB

Stang End Farm

Greenburn Beck

High Park Farm

METRES
0   500

Approximate Scale

Colwith Force
(Waterfall)

Sawrey's Wood

Start & Finish

Eltermere Country House Hotel

Elterwater [P]

Low Colwith

Elterwater is the smallest of Lakeland's sixteen lakes. Slowly it is being infilled as silt deposits encourage reed growth.

A593

Cumbria Way

Park Farm

Elter Water

Great Langdale Beck

Cumbria Way

B5343

Elterwater is a Norse name meaning 'lake of swans'. It is a haunt of a wide variety of waterfowl. The whooper swan is a winter visitor.

Skelwith Force
(Waterfall)

FB

Skelwith Bridge

Ash woodland around Elterwater were coppiced between 1824 to 1920 for the gunpowder mill, north of the village. Gunpowder was used in local quarrying.

Loughrigg Tarn

River Brathay

A593

WALK 11

41

© Crown Copyright

right of Stang End Farm. Emerge through a field-gate onto a lane.

■ **9** Turn left between the farmhouse and buildings. Go ahead, up the lane, for 400m.

■ **10** Turn left through a field-gate at a bridleway signpost. Enter the yard of High Park Farm. Go ahead between farm buildings. Turn right.

■ **11** Immediately turn left through a field-gate to leave the farmyard. Bear diagonally right, uphill, over meadowland with scattered rocky outcrops. Pass through a field-gate. Turn left along a wall on the left. Pass through a field-gate into woodland.

■ **12** Immediately turn left at a ground-level sign on the permissive path to Colwith Force. Go downhill through woodland on a path which leads to Colwith Force.

■ **13** Turn right. Take the left fork downhill. Follow the River Brathay on the left through woodland. Go past a stile on the left on arriving at a road bridge. Proceed for another 10m after the stile.

■ **14** Turn left over another stile and descend stone steps. Turn right along a road for 100m.

■ **15** Turn left over a stile at a signpost to Skelwith Bridge. Descend stone steps. Bear right over grassland to enter a wood via a stile. Ascend a short steep zig-zagging path onto a ridge. Cross over a stile. Go ahead, bending right on a path which passes over meadowland.

■ **16** Pass through a kissing-gate at the top of the path. Cross a lane. Go over a stile opposite with a wall sign to Skelwith. Proceed between high hedges. Pass over a stile to ford a rivulet. Continue ahead over meadowland.

Cross over a stile. Pass between the buildings of Park Farm. Go through the farmyard to exit through a field-gate. The broad path bends left downhill. Proceed for 80m.

■ **17** The path bends right at a signpost to Skelwith Bridge. Descend to pass through a field-gate. Continue on the path following a waymark sign. Pass through a kissing-gate. Go through the forecourt of a house on the left. Exit over a stile. Follow a driveway through a field-gate.

■ **18** Take a left fork to leave the driveway. Cross meadowland. Pass through a kissing-gate to enter a wood. Bend right at the bottom. Pass through a wicket-gate. Follow the short driveway ahead.

■ **19** Turn left onto the A593. Follow the road, downhill, bending sharply left. Cross Skelwith Bridge over the River Brathay.

■ **20** Immediately turn left at a footpath sign to Elterwater. Turn right in front of the Kirkstone Quarry Galleries to pass through the exterior tea-room area. Turn left through the quarry yard. Follow a woodland path along the River Brathay on the left for 200m.

■ **21** Bear left down a loop path to Skelwith Force. Cross a footbridge to the right. Continue right on the loop path.

■ **22** Turn left on rejoining the main path. Continue through woodland. Go through a kissing-gate. Cross meadowland.

■ **23** Go through a kissing-gate with Elter Water on the left. On emerging from the woodland, the path follows Great Langdale Beck on the left. Pass through a kissing-gate at the end of the path. Enter the car park.

BLEA TARN - SIDE PIKE - LINGMOOR FELL - BROWN HOWE

3.1 MILES (5 km)

Route Details

Distance	3.1 miles (5 km)
Degree of Difficulty	Moderate
Ascent	289m (948ft)
Time	2.5 hours

Start and Finish Points

A car park (GR 296043) on a minor road above the eastern shore of Blea Tarn. A scenic circular drive is recommended. From Ambleside take the A593 Coniston road. Just before Skelwith Bridge take the B5343 through Great Langdale. At its end, turn left onto a narrow minor road, climbing steeply before descending to Blea Tarn car park on the left. On leaving, continue on the minor road through Little Langdale. At a T-junction turn right onto another minor road. At the end, turn left on the A593 to Ambleside.

Maps Needed

OS Outdoor Leisure No 6 (1:25 000)
OS Landranger No 90 (1:50 000)

Parking Facilities

The car park (GR 296043) is the only parking space on this narrow road.

Route Description

■ **1** Start by crossing from the car park entrance. Pass through a kissing-gate adjacent to a field-gate opposite. Go straight ahead on a broad path round the foot of the tarn. Pass through another kissing-gate into mixed woodland. Go down a slope to cross a footbridge.

■ **2** Turn right to follow a terraced path. Pass through mixed woodland containing clumps of rhododendrons parallel to the west shore of the tarn down to the right. Gradually the path bends left away from the tarn.

■ **3** Pass through a kissing-gate to emerge from the woodland. Follow a stony uphill path along the lower fellside with a wall to the right. Keep climbing gradually, bending left up the fell away from the wall.

■ **4** Pass through a wall gap on a col. Turn right to emerge onto a road. Cross the road. Go over the ladder-stile opposite. Ignore the footpath sign pointing left. Go straight ahead for 40m, fording a shallow beck.

■ **5** Turn right through a wall gap. Follow a terraced path through bracken, contouring the lower fellside of Side Pike up on the left and parallel to the road

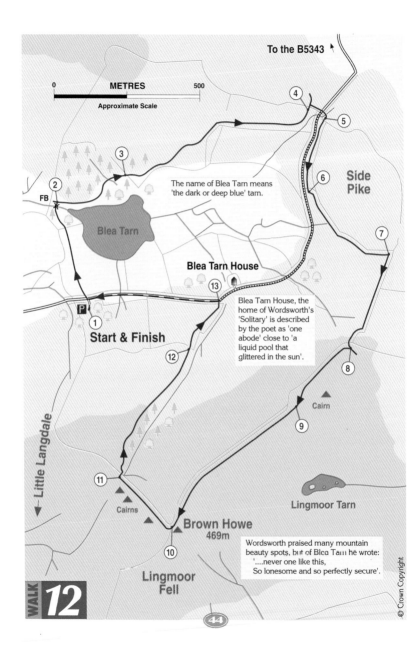

The name of Blea Tarn means 'the dark or deep blue' tarn.

Blea Tarn House

Blea Tarn House, the home of Wordsworth's 'Solitary' is described by the poet as 'one abode' close to 'a liquid pool that glittered in the sun'.

Start & Finish

To the B5343

Side Pike

Blea Tarn

FB

P

Little Langdale

Cairn

Lingmoor Tarn

Cairns

Brown Howe
469m

Lingmoor Fell

Wordsworth praised many mountain beauty spots, but of Blea Tarn he wrote:
'....never one like this,
So lonesome and so perfectly secure'.

0   METRES   500
Approximate Scale

© Crown Copyright

WALK 12

Lovely Blea Tarn backed by the rugged height of Side Pike and Lingmoor Fell

below to the right. Cross a stile in a wire fence after 350m.

■ **6** Turn left alongside the wire fence on the left which has replaced the wall. Climb the lower slopes of Side Pike up on the left.

■ **7** Turn right where the fence meets a wall ahead. Gradually ascend a grassy path along the wall on the left. It bends left round a rocky outcrop. Cross a stile at a wall corner on the left.

■ **8** Immediately turn right, ascending quite steeply up the path along the wall on the right. Bear up left after 200m away from the wall. Pass over a cairned rocky knoll.

■ **9** Continue ahead to rejoin the wall and a parallel wire fence on the right. Gradually ascend the escarpment of Lingmoor Fell with Lingmoor Tarn below on the left and Blea Tarn below on the right. Climb gradually to the

summit cairn of Brown Howe (469m/1538ft).

■ **10** Turn right from the summit cairn to cross a stile in a wire fence. Follow down the cairned path along a wall on the right. Proceed for 200m down to the bottom of the gradual slope.

■ **11** Turn right over a stile on a narrow grassy col at the head of a wooded ravine. Bear up left through a cluster of larches. Bend right, descending the grassy ridge on a meandering path marked by the occasional cairn. It runs parallel to the ravine down on the right.

■ **12** Go through a wall gap. Continue ahead down the grassy slope to emerge onto a narrow minor road with Bleatarn House 100m ahead.

■ **13** Turn left along the road. Proceed for 450m to arrive at the car park on the left.

GLEN MARY - TARN HOWS - TOM HEIGHTS - ROSE CASTLE PLANTATION

3.1 MILES (5 km)

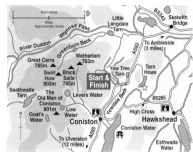

Route Details

Distance	3.1 miles (5 km)
Degree of Difficulty	Easy
Ascent	180m (590ft)
Time	2.5 hours

Start and Finish Points

Parking areas at Glen Mary Bridge (GR 322998), off the A593 Coniston to Ambleside road.

Maps Needed

OS Outdoor Leisure No 7 (1:25 000)
OS Landranger No 90 (1:50 000)
OS Landranger No 96 (1:50 000)

Parking Facilities

If the parking areas at Glen Mary Bridge (GR 322998) are full, there are two alternative car parks south of Tarn Hows. Go to Coniston. Go east on the B5285 Hawkshead road. After 2 miles (3.2km) at High Cross fork left. Turn left at the next junction. There is a car park (GR 329993) on the left and, 600m ahead, a second car park (GR 326995) also on the left. The circular walk could begin at (13) with (1) to (4) as an optional extra.

Route Description

■ **1** Start from the parking area. Cross a footbridge over Glen Mary Beck upstream of the road bridge. Turn right on an uphill path through woodland, keeping the beck on the right as the path bends left.

■ **2** Take a right fork with a waterfall up on the right. Go to the top of the falls. Continue ahead along the beck on the right.

■ **3** Fork right at a low-level sign at the top of the rise. Go down towards the steep drop of Glen Mary Waterfall. Continue past the falls on the right to ascend to the top of them. Veer left up a rocky path to pass through a wicket-gate. Continue with the stream to the right. Emerge from Glen Mary at the dammed outlet of Tarn Hows.

■ **4** Turn left on a broad lakeside path with the tarn on the right. Proceed for 225m.

■ **5** Turn left at the corner of a wire fence and a plantation on the right. Leave the lakeshore path on an uphill path through scattered trees. It twists right near the top onto the summit of a rock-capped knoll.

■ **6** From the summit continue ahead along the undulating ridge, passing over two further cairned rocky outcrops

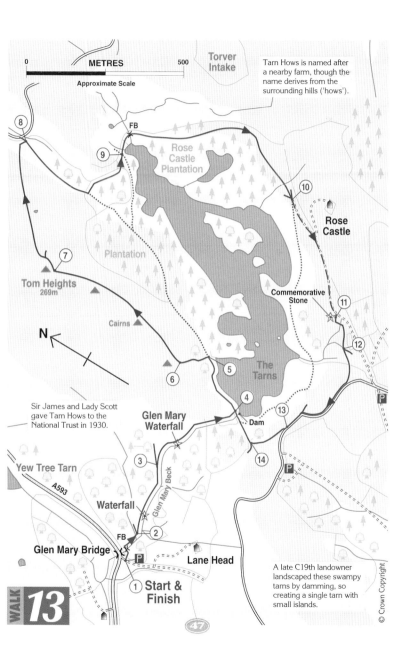

METRES
0   500

Approximate Scale

Torver
Intake

Tarn Hows is named after
a nearby farm, though the
name derives from the
surrounding hills ('hows').

⑧

FB

⑨

Rose
Castle
Plantation

Plantation

⑩

Rose
Castle

⑦

Tom Heights
269m

Cairns

Commemorative
Stone

⑪

⑫

N

⑥

⑤

The
Tarns

④

⑬

Dam

P

Sir James and Lady Scott
gave Tarn Hows to the
National Trust in 1930.

Glen Mary
Waterfall

③

Glen Mary Beck

⑭

P

Yew Tree Tarn

A593

Waterfall

②

FB

Glen Mary Bridge

P

Lane Head

① Start &
Finish

A late C19th landowner
landscaped these swampy
tarns by damming, so
creating a single tarn with
small islands.

© Crown Copyright

WALK
13

47

The ever-popular tree-enshrouded Tarn Hows and its islets

before reaching the summit cairn of Tom Heights (269m/882ft).

■ **7** Descend half-right from the summit cairn. Pass to the right of a cairned knoll, ignoring a right fork. Continue ahead, downhill, on a narrow path, passing a pond on the right. The path bends sharp right with a lane in sight behind a wall. Scramble down a short rock step to a stile and field-gate which provides access to the lane.

■ **8** Do not cross the stile onto the lane. Turn right along a broad path. Pass through a conifer plantation. Ford a rivulet. Bend left to filter onto a path coming in from the right.

■ **9** Turn left at a junction with the tarn on the right. Pass through a kissing-gate to emerge from woodland. Follow along a wire fence on the left to cross over a footbridge. Bend right making a gradual ascent into Rose Castle Plantation.

■ **10** Bear up left at cross-paths on a high level path on emerging from the plantation. Filter right at the top of the

rise onto a broad path coming in from the left. Proceed for another 200m. Bear right, off the main path, to a rocky outcrop topped by a commemorative stone on the right.

■ **11** Drop down half-left from the summit onto a grassy path, bending round right on the ridge. Ford a shallow rivulet.

■ **12** Fork left with a rocky outcrop on the right. Bend right, downhill, to cross a stile in a wire fence. Go straight ahead to join the road ahead. Do not cross the road.

■ **13** Bear right to follow a grassy path over a rolling grassy hillock. Gradually descend half-right from the grassy ridge towards the shore of the tarn to join a path coming in from the right.

■ **14** Filter right onto a path coming from the left. Pass over a stile adjacent to a field-gate. Go ahead, along the shoreline, passing over the dam wall to (4). Turn left. Follow the outward route down Glen Mary to return to the parking-areas.

WALK 14

FLASS TARN - RIVER IRT - LOW WOOD - WAST WATER

5 MILES (8 km)

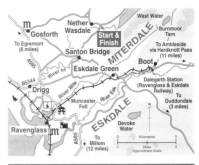

Route Details

Distance	5 miles (8 km)
Degree of Difficulty	Easy
Ascent	86m (282ft)
Time	3 hours

Start and Finish Points

Parking spaces on the verges of a triangle of land bordered by roads (GR 129038), 500m south-east of the village of Nether Wasdale.
From the A595, the west coast road, turn inland at Gosforth on a minor road east to Nether Wasdale.

Maps Needed

OS Outdoor Leisure No 6 (1:25 000)
OS Landranger No 89 (1:50 000)

Parking Facilities

There is only verge parking (GR 129038). If there are no spaces, parking in Nether Wasdale is very restricted. An alternative is to drive further east on the minor road where there is roadside parking on the western shore of Wast Water. Start and finish the walk at (14) (GR 148048).

Route Description

■ **1** Start on the western boundary road between Cinderdale Bridge and Forest Bridge. Turn left to cross Forest Bridge, following the road signposted to Santon Bridge. Go past the sign to Lakefoot where the road bends right. Proceed for another 20m.

■ **2** Turn left through a wicket-gate at a bridleway sign to Eskdale. Follow along a wire fence fringing a house on the left. Continue ahead over meadowland at the end of the fence. Cross a stile adjacent to a field-gate.

■ **3** Ford the outlet stream from Flass Tarn on the right. Ascend along the wall on the left. Cross a stile adjacent to a wicket-gate. Follow up a high wall on the left and a conifer plantation on the right. Ignore any right forks.

■ **4** Bear left with the wall on the left at a junction with a forest track.

■ **5** Keep left along the wall at a pathway junction. Pass over a stile adjacent to a field-gate. Continue ahead, descending towards Easthwaite Farm below on the left.

■ **6** Fork right at a bankside hollow on the right above the farm. Traverse the fellside on a bracken-fringed terraced path.

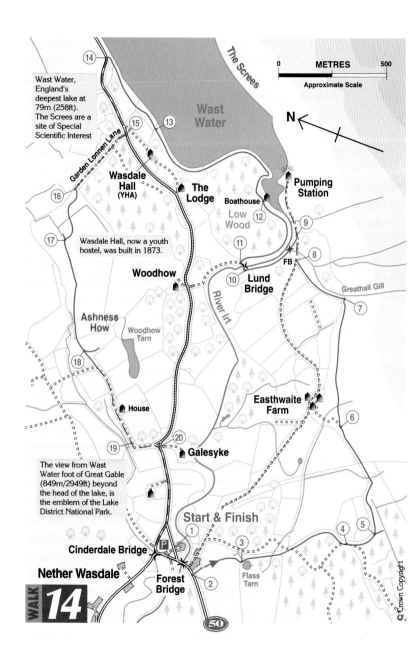

Wast Water, England's deepest lake at 79m (258ft). The Screes are a site of Special Scientific Interest

Wasdale Hall, now a youth hostel, was built in 1873.

The view from Wast Water foot of Great Gable (849m/2949ft) beyond the head of the lake, is the emblem of the Lake District National Park.

The Screes

METRES   500
Approximate Scale

N

Wast Water

Garden Lonnen Lane

Wasdale Hall (YHA)

The Lodge

Boathouse

Pumping Station

Low Wood

Woodhow

River Irt

Lund Bridge

FB

Greathall Gill

Ashness How

Woodhow Tarn

Easthwaite Farm

House

Galesyke

Start & Finish

Cinderdale Bridge

Nether Wasdale

Forest Bridge

Flass Tarn

P

© Crown Copyright

WALK 14

50

■ **7** Turn left over a stile at a wall corner. Go downhill along Greathall Gill on the right. Cross a stile adjacent to a field-gate at the bottom of the slope.

■ **8** Turn right on a downhill path.

Great Gable, left, high above Wast Water

■ **9** Pass through a kissing-gate adjacent to a field-gate. Continue ahead for 250m on a gravelled track as far as the Pumping-Station for views of the Wast Water Screes. Retrace the outward route to (9). Branch right 20m after the gate at a ground-level sign to Wasdale. Follow the River Irt on the right, crossing a footbridge. Pass through a kissing-gate ahead. Continue along the riverbank to go through a kissing-gate.

■ **10** Turn right over Lund Bridge. Immediately go through a field-gate. Proceed for 6m.

■ **11** Turn right through a kissing-gate into woodland. Go right to follow the ground-level sign to the lakeshore/YHA. Follow the course of the river to a boathouse.

■ **12** Turn left round the southern shore of Wast Water. Emerge from the wood through a field-gate. Continue ahead along the lakeshore, passing below the YHA Wasdale Hall up on the left.

■ **13** Pass through a kissing-gate into a small wood. Emerge from woodland through a fence gap. Cross pastureland. Pass through rhododendrons. Ascend steps to cross over a high ladder-stile. Turn left up the bank to the junction with the road.

■ **14** Turn left up the road. Pass through a field-gate adjacent to a cattle-grid. Proceed for 250m.

■ **15** Turn right, off the road, at a footpath sign. Go up Garden Lonnen Lane with a high-walled garden on the right. Continue ahead where the wall ends with a wood on the left. Cross over a ladder-stile adjacent to a field-gate at the end of the wood.

■ **16** Bear half-left on a rutted path over grassland, contouring right round a rocky outcrop. Bend left round another outcrop up to a signpost ahead.

■ **17** Turn left on a winding broad path over open fell. Keep straight ahead, ignoring any branch paths. Pass over a stile adjacent to a field-gate. Continue ahead.

■ **18** Go ahead at a fence corner ahead on the left with a signpost left to Woodhow. Pass over a stile adjacent to a field-gate. Follow ahead the bridleway sign to Galesyke. Pass over another stile adjacent to a field-gate. Continue ahead, immediately passing a house on the left. Go over another stile adjacent to a field-gate and continue ahead.

■ **19** Cross a stile adjacent to a field-gate. Immediately the track bends left. Emerge onto a road.

■ **20** Turn right along the road. Proceed for 400m to return to the parking area on the left.

**RAVENGLASS -
WALLS CASTLE -
MUNCASTER CASTLE -
BEACH**

4.5 MILES (7.2 km)

Route Details

Distance	4.5 miles (7.2 km)
Degree of Difficulty	Easy
Ascent	90m (295ft)
Time	3 hours

Start and Finish Points

Ravenglass car park (GR 085964)
behind The Ratty Arms.
From the A595, the west coast road, at
a major right-angle turn, go seawards
west, down a minor road at a sign post
to Ravenglass. The car park is on the left
beyond the railway bridges.

Maps Needed

OS Outdoor Leisure No 6 (1:25 000)
OS Landranger No 96 (1:50 000)

Parking Facilities

The large Ravenglass car park (GR
085964) not only has access to main-
line trains, but also to the narrow-guage
Ravenglass and Eskdale Railway and its
museum from where a scenic train
journey up the Esk Valley can be taken.
Muncaster Castle and its gardens can be
visited en route.

Route Description

■ **1** Start by leaving the car park from
the opposite corner from the
entrance. Cross the footbridge over
the railway line. Go half-left across
the corner of a playing-field. Pass
between gate-posts on a short path.
Emerge onto a lane.
■ **2** Turn right at a sign to Newtown
Knott/Muncaster. Pass Walls Castle, the
Roman bath-house on the left. Proceed
for another 150m.
■ **3** Turn left at a fork to follow another
lane. It ascends gradually, eventually
bending right, then left. Go beneath
national grid power-lines. Proceed for
another 200m.
■ **4** Turn sharp left in a clump of
rhododendrons at a footpath sign. The
broad path climbs gradually through
woodland along a stream. Pass through
a field-gate to emerge from the
woodland onto open grassland.
Continue ahead to cross a stile adjacent
to a field-gate. Go through a field-gate at
the end of the park.
■ **5** Turn left up a wooded lane. Enter
the yard of Home Farm. Bear right
through the farmyard onto the driveway
which emerges on the A595.
■ **6** Cross the road and turn right.

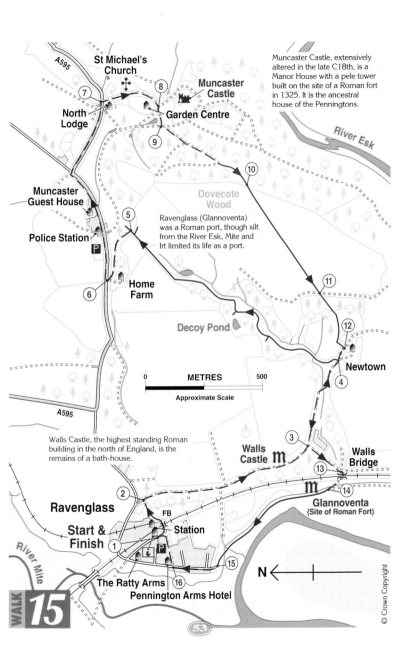

Muncaster Castle, extensively altered in the late C18th, is a Manor House with a pele tower built on the site of a Roman fort in 1325. It is the ancestral house of the Penningtons.

St Michael's Church

Muncaster Castle

Garden Centre

North Lodge

Muncaster Guest House

Police Station

Home Farm

Dovecote Wood

Ravenglass (Glannoventa) was a Roman port, though silt from the River Esk, Mite and Irt limited its life as a port.

River Esk

Decoy Pond

Newtown

METRES
0   500
Approximate Scale

A595

A595

Walls Castle, the highest standing Roman building in the north of England, is the remains of a bath-house.

Walls Castle ⋔

Walls Bridge

Ravenglass

Start & Finish

Station

FB

Glannoventa
(Site of Roman Fort)

The Ratty Arms

Pennington Arms Hotel

N ←

© Crown Copyright

WALK **15**

53

River Mite

Continue on the roadside pavement. Pass a car park on the left opposite the West Lodge entrance-gate to Muncaster Castle. The road passes, on the left, the Police Station and the old school, now Muncaster Guest House. It begins to ascend before taking a sharp right bend to the top of a rise, then continues downhill.

■ **7** Turn right to cross the road at the bottom of the hill at a footpath sign to Muncaster Church/Ravenglass. Go between stone gate-posts with North Lodge on the right to enter the grounds of Muncaster Castle. Continue along the driveway, passing St Michael's Church on the left. The driveway bends right, passing a garden centre on the right. Go between a high wall and the estate offices.

■ **8** Turn right at a junction with the castle over to the left. Follow the footpath sign for 20m. Turn left off the walkway at a footpath sign on a fence-post on the left. Follow the path with the wire fence and a duckpond on the right. Keep ahead across the lawns through a children's playing-area.

■ **9** Turn left at a junction. Turn right after 20m at a footpath sign to Ravenglass via Newtown. Follow an uphill woodland track.

■ **10** Pass over a fence via stone steps adjacent to a wicket-gate. Emerge from the castle grounds onto open grassland. Follow the line of the footpath sign to Ravenglass via Newtown on a faint path. Keep on the level over grassland to pass over a shallow shoulder of a grassy knoll to the left. Keep aiming for the estuary mouth ahead and an electricity pylon in the middle-ground.

■ **11** Cross a stile over a wire fence at the bottom of the slope. The narrow meandering downhill path continues through a plantation. Go through a wicket-gate onto a lane at the foot of the descent.

■ **12** Turn right on the lane. Proceed to (4) and follow the outward route. At (3) turn left on a lane where on the left a low sign indicates the shore/Ravenglass/Brighouse Farm.

■ **13** Turn right at a junction after 200m on the downhill lane. Pass under a railway bridge to emerge onto the stony beach.

Delightful Muncaster Castle and its gardens

■ **14** Turn right and follow the high-water mark. (If high tides go back to (3) and retrace the outward route). Proceed for 700m with eroding cliffs on the right eventually giving way to houses.

■ **15** Turn right at a wall corner up a slipway through entrance gates to the beach. Go straight ahead for 200m along the main street of Ravenglass.

■ **16** Turn right immediately before the Pennington Arms Hotel at a lamp-post bearing a footpath sign to the Railway Station. Pass between buildings into the car park.

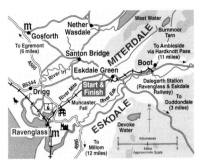

MITERDALE - BURNMOOR TARN - RAVENGLASS & ESKDALE RAILWAY

6.5 MILES (10.5 km)

Route Details

Distance	6.5 miles (10.5 km)
Degree of Difficulty	Moderate
Ascent	220m (722ft)
Time	4.5 hours

Start and Finish Points

Irton Road Station (GR 138999) car park on the Ravenglass and Eskdale Railway.
The walk is from Irton Road Station up Miterdale and down to Boot in Eskdale to Dalegarth Station (GR 173007), the narrow-guage railway terminus. From here take the train ('The Ratty') on a scenic journey down Eskdale. Alight at Irton Road Station.

Maps Needed

OS Outdoor Leisure No 6 (1:25 000)
OS Landranger No 89 (1:50 000)
OS Landranger No 96 (1:50 000)

Parking Facilities

The car park at Irton Road Station (GR 138999) is the only parking space near the start of the walk, and the obvious finish point for the railway journey.

Route Description

■ **1** Start from the car park entrance. Filter right onto a lane. Filter left onto the road. Proceed for 100m.

■ **2** Turn right over the road. Opposite, follow a narrow tarmac lane, initially between houses. Pass a school on the left. Continue on the road for 1.2 miles (4km).

■ **3** Pass through a field-gate. Continue along the lane over cross-tracks. Go through a field-gate ahead.

■ **4** Fork left, off the road, crossing diagonally over a car park. Turn left over a footbridge at a bridleway sign to Wasdale Head.

■ **5** Immediately fork right. Follow a broad uphill path away from the river. Filter right at a bridleway junction. Proceed for 0.6 miles (1km). Enter the yard of Low Place Farm through a field-gate. Go between farm buildings.

■ **6** Turn right through a field-gate at the end of the farmyard at a bridleway sign to Wasdale. Follow round a wall on the left for 100m.

■ **7** Turn right over a gated footbridge over the River Irt. Immediately bear left up a broad path over open fell. Pass through two field-gates. Keep ahead, gradually ascending with a conifer

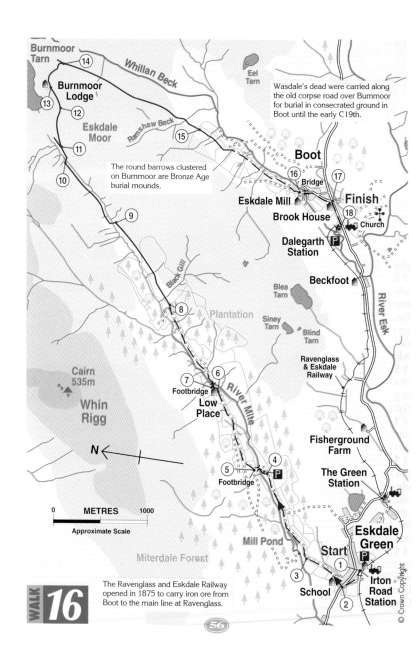

Burnmoor
Tarn

Whillan Beck

Eel
Tarn

(14)

Burnmoor
Lodge

(13)

(12)

Eskdale
Moor

Ramshaw Beck

Wasdale's dead were carried along
the old corpse road over Burnmoor
for burial in consecrated ground in
Boot until the early C19th.

(11)

(15)

Boot

(10)

The round barrows clustered
on Burnmoor are Bronze Age
burial mounds.

(16)

Bridge

(17)

Finish

Eskdale Mill

(9)

Brook House

(18)

Church

Dalegarth
Station

Beckfoot

Black Gill

(8)

Plantation

Blea
Tarn

Siney
Tarn

Blind
Tarn

Ravenglass
& Eskdale
Railway

River Esk

Cairn
535m

Whin
Rigg

(7)

(6)

Footbridge

Low
Place

River Mite

N ←

Fisherground
Farm

The Green
Station

(4)

(5)

Footbridge

P

0   METRES   1000

Approximate Scale

Miterdale Forest

Eskdale
Green

Mill Pond

Start

P

(3)

(1)

Irton
Road
Station

© Crown Copyright

(2)

School

WALK

16

The Ravenglass and Eskdale Railway
opened in 1875 to carry iron ore from
Boot to the main line at Ravenglass.

56

Historic Eskdale Mill in the village of Boot

plantation on the right.

■ **8** Cross over a stile adjacent to a wicket-gate. Follow ahead at a ground-level footpath sign on the right. Ford Black Gill at a wall corner on the left. Go up the bankside, bending right through two broken walls. Cross a ladder-stile adjacent to a field-gate.

■ **9** Turn left, fording the shallow River Irt at the entrance to a ravine. Turn right to go upstream with the river on the right.

■ **10** Turn right, fording the river at the narrowest point of the ravine. Turn left to go upstream with the river on the left.

■ **11** Bear right at a fork near the top of the ravine. Climb away from the river above a combe below on the left. The path becomes indistinct, but bear right uphill to avoid boggy ground, making for a clean-cut bracken-line round the base of the hills.

■ **12** Bear left along the bracken-line on the right on a thin terraced path which contours round right with Burnmoor Tarn down below on the left. Continue to Burnmoor Lodge.

■ **13** Turn right from the lodge on a flat path, bending left round a hillock on the right. Bear right uphill as far as a junction.

■ **14** Filter right onto an old corpse road. The broad cairned path bends right, uphill, then descends, bending left to ford Ramshaw Beck. Ahead, pass through a field-gate.

■ **15** Follow along a wall on the left. Go through two field-gates. Go ahead through a wicket-gate. Continue downhill along a wall to the left. Pass through a wall gap near the bottom. Bear left down a path round an S-bend. Follow the bridleway sign ahead to pass through a field-gate. Go down a short walled lane to a narrow road.

■ **16** Continue ahead on the road. Cross a humpbacked bridge. Keep ahead on the road through Boot.

Burnmoor Tarn at the head of Miterdale

■ **17** Turn right at a road junction. Stay on the road for 250m.

■ **18** Turn right into Dalegarth Station. Take 'The Ratty' train on the Ravenglass and Eskdale Railway back to Irton Road Station.

WALK 17

MUNCASTER FELL - RAVENGLASS & ESKDALE RAILWAY - MUNCASTER MILL

5.5 MILES (8.9 km)

Route Details

Distance	5.5 miles (8.9 km)
Degree of Difficulty	Moderate
Ascent	201m (659ft)
Time	4 hours

Start and Finish Points

The car park (GR 097967) on the A595 near Ravenglass is opposite the entrance to Muncaster Castle. From here walk over Muncaster Fell and down to Irton Road Station (GR138999) at (10). Catch the train ('The Ratty') west towards Ravenglass on the narrow-guage railway. Alight at Muncaster Mill (GR 096977) at (11). Walk up to the car park.

Maps Needed

OS Outdoor Leisure No 6 (1:25 000)
OS Landranger No 96 (1:50 000)

Parking Facilities

The car park (GR 097967) may be used by kind permission of Muncaster Estates. It is opposite the entrance to Muncaster Castle and close by is Muncaster Mill adjacent to the station. Both are open to the public and on the walk route.

Route Description

■ **1** Start from the car park. Turn left up the A595 for 400m.

■ **2** Go straight ahead where the road bends sharply right. Follow a bridleway signpost to Eskdale and Hardknott up the walled Fell Lane. Pass through a field-gate. Continue ahead uphill.

■ **3** Go through a wicket-gate adjacent to the middle of three field-gates. Pass Muncaster Tarn through the trees on the left. Continue ahead uphill. Go through a kissing-gate at the top of the rise. Proceed ahead over open fell, ignoring branch paths.

■ **4** Fork left, off the path, up a bankside at a plantation corner on the left. A narrow loop path meanders up to the OS triangulation pillar and cairn on the summit of Hooker Crag (231m/758ft).

■ **5** Go ahead from the cairn for 20m. Turn sharp right. Follow a downhill path, bending left. Cross a depression to join the main path.

■ **6** Turn left, bending right round a broad marshy area on the left. The boggy path rises gradually between rocky outcrops. Continue to a huge flat stone table at Ross's Camp.

■ **7** Go ahead on a broad downhill path

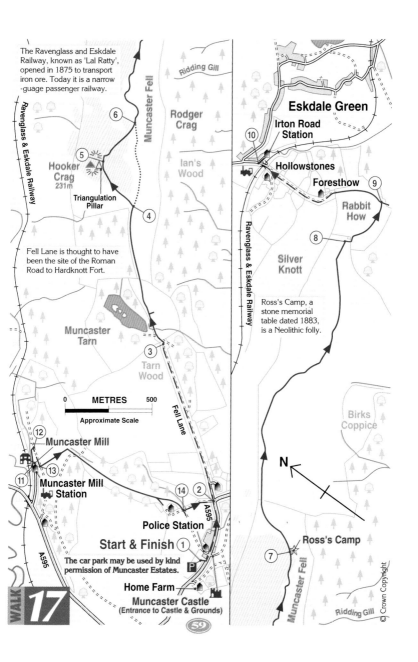

The Ravenglass and Eskdale Railway, known as 'Lal Ratty', opened in 1875 to transport iron ore. Today it is a narrow-guage passenger railway.

Ridding Gill

Ravenglass & Eskdale Railway

Muncaster Fell

Rodger Crag

Ian's Wood

⑥

⑤

Hooker Crag
231m

Triangulation Pillar

④

Eskdale Green

Irton Road Station

⑩

Hollowstones

Foresthow ⑨

Rabbit How

⑧

Fell Lane is thought to have been the site of the Roman Road to Hardknott Fort.

Silver Knott

Ravenglass & Eskdale Railway

Muncaster Tarn

③

Tarn Wood

Ross's Camp, a stone memorial table dated 1883, is a Neolithic folly.

Fell Lane

0   METRES   500

Approximate Scale

Birks Coppice

⑫

Muncaster Mill

⑬

N

⑪

Muncaster Mill Station

⑭ ②

Police Station

A595

Start & Finish ①

The car park may be used by kind permission of Muncaster Estates.

Ⓟ

Home Farm

Muncaster Castle
(Entrance to Castle & Grounds)

Ross's Camp

⑦

Muncaster Fell

Ridding Gill

A595

© Crown Copyright

WALK

17

59

'La'al Ratty' train, trundling along the floor of picturesque Eskdale valley

curving left down to a marshy depression. Bend right through a gap at a wall corner. Continue ahead along a wall on the left. The path sweeps right, away from the wall, skirting marshy ground on the left backed by Silver Knott. Go up an incline. Descend the path ahead.

■ **8** Pass through a kissing-gate adjacent to a field-gate on a narrow plateau. Continue ahead, downhill, to a pathway junction.

■ **9** Turn left on a grassy path with Rabbit How up on the left. Pass through a field-gate on approaching a white house. The path becomes a walled tarmac lane. Pass over a railway bridge.

■ **10** Turn right, down a lane leading into Irton Road Station. Catch 'The Ratty' train west to Muncaster Mill Station.

■ **11** Alight at Muncaster Mill Station. Turn left along the platform. Go uphill between the Mill buildings which are open to the public. Turn right at a footpath sign up the bankside at the water-wheel on the left.

■ **12** Turn right at the top of the rise at a bridleway sign to the castle/ Ravenglass. Proceed for 60m.

■ **13** Double back left at diagonal cross-paths. Go up a bridleway signposted to the castle. Climb through woodland. At the top of an incline the path is joined by another path from the right. Pass through a field-gate to emerge from the wood.

■ **14** Turn left at cross paths. Proceed along a wall and wood on the left, bending right. Pass through a field-gate at (2). Turn right, down the A595, to the car park on the right.

WALK 18

STANLEY FORCE -
ESK VALLEY -
DOCTOR BRIDGE -
GILL FORCE

4 MILES (6.5 km)

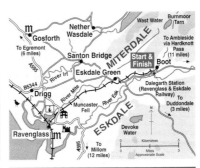

Route Details

Distance	4 miles (6.5 km)
Degree of Difficulty	Easy
Ascent	135m (443ft)
Time	3 hours

Start and Finish Points

Pay and display car park (GR 173007)
at Dalegarth Station, south-west of Boot.
It can be reached on the narrow-guage
Ravenglass and Eskdale Railway from
Ravenglass and intermediate stations.
By road, from Ambleside to the east is a
scenic journey on narrow winding roads
over Wrynose and Hardknott passes.
From the west on the A595, turn inland
and follow minor roads east from either
Gosforth via Santon Bridge and Eskdale
Green, or Holmrook via Eskdale Green.

Maps Needed

OS Outdoor Leisure No 6 (1:25 000)
OS Landranger No 89 (1:50 000)
OS Landranger No 96 (1:50 000)

Parking Facilities

Alternative parking is Trough House
Bridge car park (GR 172002).

Route Description

■ **1** Start from the entrance to the car
park. Turn right along the road for
250m.
■ **2** Turn left onto a lane at a sign to
Dalegarth Falls with the Eskdale
Outdoor Centre building on the right.
Pass a cenotaph on the right. Cross over
the road bridge. Pass Trough House
Bridge car park on the left with a sign to
Stanley Gill.
■ **3** Fork left at the lane end at a
signpost to Stanley Gill/Birker Moor
Waterfalls. Go through a field-gate. Bend
left up an incline.
■ **4** Pass over cross-paths at the top of
the rise with a wall on the left. Go
through a wicket-gate into woodland.
Continue ahead to a junction with the
riverside path.
■ **5** Turn right, upstream, with the gill
on the left. Cross over a footbridge
across a dry gill. Continue up the gorge
with the gill still on the left.
■ **6** Turn left over a stepped footbridge.
Turn right with the stream now to the
right. Turn right after 100m to re-cross
the stream over another stepped
footbridge. Continue for 20m.
■ **7** Descend to turn left over a
footbridge. Turn right up to a viewing

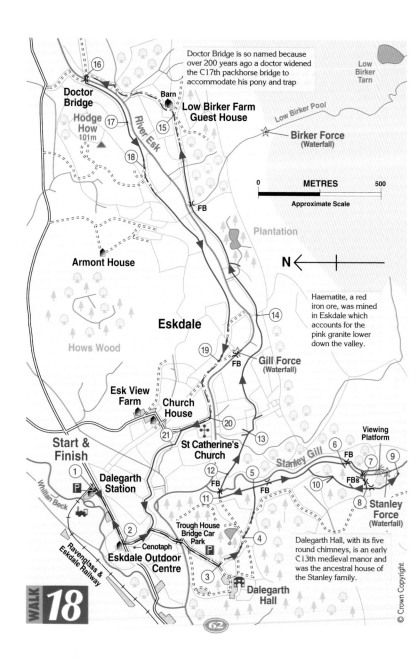

Doctor Bridge is so named because over 200 years ago a doctor widened the C17th packhorse bridge to accommodate his pony and trap

Low Birker Tarn

(16)
Doctor Bridge
(17)
Hodge How 101m
(18)

River Esk

Barn
(15)
Low Birker Farm Guest House

Low Birker Pool

Birker Force (Waterfall)

0   METRES   500
Approximate Scale

FB

Plantation

Armont House

N ←

Haematite, a red iron ore, was mined in Eskdale which accounts for the pink granite lower down the valley.

Eskdale

Hows Wood

(14)

(19)
FB
Gill Force (Waterfall)

Esk View Farm
Church House
(20)
(21)
St Catherine's Church
(13)

Stanley Gill

Viewing Platform
(6)
FB
(7)
(9)

Start & Finish

(1)
Dalegarth Station

Whillan Beck

(2)
Eskdale Outdoor Centre

Cenotaph

(12)
FB
(11)
(5)
FB

(10)
FBs
(8)
Stanley Force (Waterfall)

Trough House Bridge Car Park

(4)

(3)
Dalegarth Hall

Ravenglass & Eskdale Railway

Dalegarth Hall, with its five round chimneys, is an early C13th medieval manor and was the ancestral house of the Stanley family.

© Crown Copyright

WALK 18

62

platform. Return to (7). Go ahead, up a stairway, crossing a small footbridge and bending left.

■ **8** Turn left to cross a single-slab stone footbridge at the top of the rise. Bend right through rhododendrons. Nearing the top of the rise, bear left onto a rock platform at the head of Stanley Force. Keep away from the edge.

■ **9** Turn round and retrace the outward route as far as (8). Go straight across up a wooded footpath. Fork left, downhill, to a depression.

■ **10** Fork right on a narrow path. Turn right through a broken wall near the bottom. Turn left on the outward path to (5). Continue ahead with the gill on the right.

■ **11** Turn right, downhill, at a field-gate on the left. Cross a footbridge. Ahead, pass through a field-gate out of woodland onto grassland.

■ **12** Bear half-right through bracken to ford a shallow beck. Proceed half-right to a wall corner. Ignore the bridleway sign to the left.

■ **13** Turn left along the wall on the left. Cross over a stile adjacent to a field-gate at the next wall corner. Continue ahead with the river below on the left.

■ **14** Pass through a field-gate. Continue ahead with a wall on the left, passing a small conifer plantation enclosing a tarn on the right. Go through a field-gate at the bottom of a slope. Cross a stone-stepped footbridge over a rivulet. Continue ahead, climbing gradually up the walled path.

■ **15** Turn left at a footpath junction, passing Low Birker Farm Guest House on the right. Follow a fenced driveway bending right round a barn. Pass through a field-gate. Continue along the driveway for 150m.

■ **16** Turn left over Doctor Bridge over the River Esk. Immediately turn left at a footpath sign to St Catherine's Church. Cross over a stile adjacent to a field-gate along a path with the river on the left.

■ **17** Go through a wicket-gate. Continue on a path which bends left along the river. Proceed for 250m.

■ **18** Go ahead on a walled path at a field-gate on the left. Pass through a field-gate at the top of a rise. Continue along the riverside path. Pass through a kissing-gate. Continue ahead with the river down below on the left. Go through a field-gate.

Doctor Bridge and distant Harter Fell

■ **19** Continue ahead where a branch path leads down left to a footbridge to Gill Force. Bend left 150m ahead. Go through a kissing-gate. Follow round right with the river on the left.

■ **20** Turn right away from the river along a walled lane. Pass St Catherine's Church on the left. Proceed for 100m.

■ **21** Turn left up a walled path. Pass through a field-gate after 300m. Ahead, filter right onto the lane used on the outward route. Retrace the route via (2) back to the car park.

Walking & Safety Tips

This section is virtually the same as we publish in our Classic Walks of Discovery Series which are designed for the very serious walker, covering much longer routes on very difficult and high altitude terrain. However, the basic principles still apply so we have retained this detail for your information.

It is absolutely essential that anyone venturing out into the countryside, particularly hilly terrain, be correctly prepared to reduce the risk of injury or fatality. No amount of advice could cover all possible situations that may arise. Therefore the following walking and safety tips are not intended to be an exhaustive list, but merely a contribution from our personal experiences for your consideration.

Clothing & Equipment

The lists represent the basic equipment required to enjoy a full day's hill walking, reasonably safely and comfortably.

CLOTHING:- Strong, sensible footwear, preferably boots with a good sole, but strong trainers or lightweight boots can be worn during prolonged dry weather; warm shirt, fibre pile jacket, warm woollen sweater, windproof and waterproof hooded anorak and overtrousers (several thin layers insulate more adequately than one layer), thermal gloves; woollen hat or balaclava, warm trousers (avoid denim/jeans which become very clammy and cold when wet and could induce exposure), and good quality woollen socks or stockings, protected by waterproof gaiters.

EQUIPMENT:- Good compass and maps of the areas, along with a survival bag, whistle or torch for implementing the International Distress Signal - 6 long blasts/flashes in quick succession followed by one minute pause then repeated (the answering signal is 3 blasts or flashes). A basic first-aid kit should also be carried, which contains - bandages, sticking plasters, safety pins, scissors and some gauze pads. Take a rucksack in which to carry your equipment, and some food, plus extra food for emergency rations - chocolate, fruit cake, cheese and dried fruit. Extra liquid should be carried in hot weather.

Preparation & Procedure

Ensure that yourself and the others are adequately equipped and that no-one is overburdened. Learn how to use your map and compass competently. You should always be able to at least locate yourself on a map. Find out the weather forecasts for the area. Always consider the wind chill factor - even the gentlest of winds can reduce effective temperatures to a dangerous level. Plan both the route and possible escape routes beforehand, balancing terrain, weather forecast and the hours of daylight against experience whilst allowing for a safety margin. Always try to plan your walk so the prevailing wind is behind you. Always try to walk in company. It is safer and more enjoyable. Gain a basic understanding of first aid. Try to leave written details of your route, point of departure, number in your group, destination and estimated time of return. In an emergency this information could save a life. Maintain a steady rhythm, at the pace of the slowest walker. Take care when you are walking to avoid sprains. Be very careful where you step and remain extremely vigilant about avoiding the adder, Britain's native poisonous snake. Take regular breaks - mainly to check your progress and the next stage. Keep an eye on the weather. Always be prepared to turn back if necessary. On completion of your journey, inform the person with whom you left your written information of your safe arrival.

Stay Wise - Stay Alive

First aid on the hills requires both knowledge and common sense. If in doubt concentrate on the comfort and morale of the casualty. **IN AN EMERGENCY: STOP AND THINK - DO NOT PANIC**. If you are lost - check your surroundings carefully and try and locate yourself on your map. Find shelter and decide whether it is safe or best to use an escape route. If someone is injured, or is showing the signs of exposure (i.e. stumbling and slurred speech, shivering, irrational behaviour or collapse and unconsciousness) **STOP IMMEDIATELY**, prevent further heat loss, find shelter and place the casualty into a survival bag with extra clothing. Huddle together as a group and give the casualty some warm food and drink. **DO NOT**: rub the casualty, give alcohol, allow further exposure. Decide then on your next course of action. Do you go for help? or do you stay put overnight sending out the International Distress Signal? If you have to stay put overnight try and find or make adequate shelter, conserve food and drink, keep morale high, keep the casualty warm, dry and conscious, and use the International Distress Signal. If you are able to leave someone with the casualty whilst two of your party go for help from a village or farm the following information is essential; accurate location of the casualty, nature of injuries, number injured, number in group, condition of others in group (if one person is suffering it is possible that others will be too), treatment already given, and time of accident. Remember that **WET + COLD = EXPOSURE**. This rapid cooling of the inner body can lead to fatalities. **ALWAYS BE PREPARED.**

Tourist Information

(**NP**) = National Park. (**S**) = Seasonal.
AMBLESIDE (S)
The Old Courthouse, Church Street.
Tel: (015394) 32582
AMBLESIDE
National Trust, Rothay Holme, Rothay Rd.
Tel: (015394) 35599
BARROW-IN-FURNESS
Forum 28, Duke Street.
Tel: (01229) 870156
BOWNESS-ON-WINDERMERE (S)
Glebe Road.
Tel: (015394) 42895
CONISTON (S)
16 Yewdale Road.
Tel: (015394) 41533
EGREMONT
Lowes Court Gallery, 12 Main Street.
Tel: (01946) 820693
GLENRIDDING (NP) (S)
Main Car Park.
Tel: (017684) 82414
GRANGE-OVER-SANDS (S)
Victoria Hall, Main Street.
Tel: (015395) 34026
GRASMERE (NP) (S)
Red Bank Road.
Tel: (015394) 35245
GRASMERE
National Trust Information Centre,
Church Stile. Tel: (015394) 35621
HAWKSHEAD (S)
Main Car Park.
Tel: (015394) 36525
KENDAL
Town Hall, Highgate.
Tel: (01539) 725758
MILLOM (S)
Millom Folk Museum
Tel: (01229) 772555

SEATOLLER (NP) (S)
Seatoller Barn, Borrowdale.
Tel: (017687) 77294
ULVERSTON
Coronation Hall, County Square.
Tel: (01229) 587120
WATERHEAD (S)
The Car Park.
Tel: (015394) 32729
WINDERMERE
Victoria Street.
Tel: (015394) 46499
WHITEHAVEN
Market Hall, Market Place.
Tel: (01946) 695678

Useful Information

FELL RESCUE SERVICES
Contact the Police. Tel: 999
WEATHER FORECAST
National Park recorded information
(including details of fell-top
conditions)
Tel: (017687) 75757
RADIO CUMBRIA
Frequencies: medium 397 (North),
358 (Central & South), 206 (West),
VHF 104.2 (Central) and
95 - 96 (all other areas).
**LONG DISTANCE WALKERS
ASSOCIATION**
117 Higher Lane, Rainford,
St Helens, Merseyside,
WA11 8BQ.
Tel: (01744) 882638
THE DISCOVERY VISITOR CENTRE
1 Market Place, Middleton-in-
Teesdale, Co Durham, DL12 OQG
Tel & Fax: (01833) 640638
For details of current and forthcoming
Walks of Discovery walking guides.

CU00406463

Wainwright: The Podcasts

CD tracks

Wainwright:
The Podcasts

Introduced by
Eric Robson

Read by
Nik Wood-Jones

FRANCES LINCOLN LIMITED
PUBLISHERS

Frances Lincoln Limited, 4 Torriano Mews,
Torriano Avenue, London NW5 2RZ
www.franceslincoln.com

The Pictorial Guides to the Lakeland Fells first published by
Frances Lincoln 2003
This collection published by Frances Lincoln in association with
Cumbria Tourism 2008

SAFETY
Fell walking can be **dangerous**, especially in wet, windy, foggy or icy
conditions. Read the **Safety Note** at the end of this book, and always
take sensible precautions when out on the fells.

PUBLISHER'S NOTE
All maps, walks and instructions included here have been revised
and updated by Chris Jesty. They were correct, to the best of our
knowledge, at the time of publication in 2008. Nonetheless, routes
suggested on the CD may occasionally vary from routes shown in this
book, and walkers need to be clear which route they are following.

Printed and bound in Slovenia
A CIP catalogue record is available for this book from the British Library

ISBN 978 0 7112 2984 8

9 8 7 6 5 4 3 2 1

Contents

Introduction

The year was 1778. The place, Sizergh Castle, near Kendal. A man, seen by the light of a sputtering candle to be dressed as a Jesuit priest, set aside his quill pen and looked through the manuscript he'd just completed. It had taken Father Thomas West three years to write his *Guide to the Lakes*. Three years during which he had ridden back and forth across a 'parish' that stretched from Furness to Kendal to Workington. He'd gathered the information for the guide as a hobby, something to take the edge off the long hours in the saddle involved in being a Riding priest, ministering to the scattered Roman Catholic populations of what was known as the Manor Mission of Furness. As he re-read the pages he'd written, Father West knew he'd devised a useful new style of book, but what he couldn't know, that evening in 1778, was that his hobby would lay the foundations of the most successful visitor destination in Britain.

Now, it may seem an uncomfortably long jump from a guidebook-writing Jesuit priest two-and-a-bit centuries ago to a podcast downloadable from cyberspace. But in fact they're both part of an honourable tradition of landscape interpretation. In their own way, they both attempt to make sense of scenery which, you may be surprised to hear, unlike death and taxes has not always been with us. In fact the very word *scenery*, as related to landscape rather than stage sets, according to the OED dates from as late as 1777, the year before the first edition of West's guide.

In the forty or so years after the publication of

West's book, the number of tourists to the Lake District increased dramatically. And as the number of visitors went up, local people began to spot business opportunities. Visitors needed guides to get them to the best viewpoints as they went in search of the picturesque. The fashion of the time said that the novice visitor needed assistance; should go warily, clutching a Claude glass (a sort of tinted convex mirror in which they would see a reflection of the landscape). This new-fangled scenery was powerful stuff. Too powerful to look on directly. The mountains were regarded as a fearsome waste – a land where lurked all manner of horrors. Professionals who knew the lie of that land and could bring their charges safely home from it were suddenly much in demand, as they had been for years in the Alps. In fact, at the time, the Lake District was being sold as the training slopes for those who planned Alpine adventures. And in a distant echo of the impact of international terrorism on modern overseas travel, Continental wars at the beginning of the nineteenth century encouraged people to explore landscapes closer to home.

A reminder of those pioneering tourist days can be found at Lakeland gatherings such as Grasmere sports, where they still hold guide races. Today they are fell running fixtures, but originally they would have been events in which the district's mountain guides could show off their virility to potential customers.

And in the last couple of hundred years, guiding has flourished in all manner of ways. There's a direct line of descent from Thomas West to the many companies that now offer guided walking tours in the Lake District and elsewhere. There's never been a better choice of mountain mapping for sensible, independent walkers who arm themselves with map and compass (and take the time and trouble to learn how to use them). There are the mapping systems on CD Rom that allow walkers to pre-plan their own routes into the hills and sample the views from the comfort of their own desktop computer. Systems like this may have set back Father West in amazement but for the IT literate they are a natural extension of walking boots. Then there's GPS, that wonderful gadget that sends articulated lorries over Hardknott Pass and leaves unwary walkers needing mountain rescue assistance when its battery goes down somewhere on Scafell. And palmtop computers that can tell you where you were twenty minutes ago, where you should be in twenty minutes and in the meantime, in case you happen to be bored on Bowfell, will also advertise the range of mountain books available on Amazon. There are mountain weather forecasts you can pick up on your mobile phone and webcams that will show you what the weather's like at Wasdale Head before you set off from home. (Whether it's the same when you get there will be anybody's guess. It's often not the same when I get there and I only live six miles down the valley.) And then there are podcasts, more of which anon.

But still dominating the guiding market all these years later, there are the guidebooks themselves. Thousands of them. Fat, thin, glossy, dowdy, cheap as chips, overpriced. A guidebook for every mood and every pocket. Most should probably never have been written. I know that because I've written guidebooks that should never have been written – guidebooks tempted into life by vanity or fifteen pieces of silver (the market's not as lucrative these days).

The problem with most guidebooks is that they miss the point. They think that 'turn left here, mind the drop on your right, the footpath's badly eroded and it should take you an hour and a half to the top' is what guidebooks should be about. Proper guidebooks should have a more substantial core if they're to join the library of greats. They should be opinionated. They should impart knowledge, local knowledge, knowledge hard won by experiencing the landscape and thinking about it and interpreting it and setting it into context. Not simply describing it.

They need a bit of Wordsworthian fulmination. His *Guide to the Lakes*, the first edition of which was published in 1810, thirty odd years after Thomas West set the ball rolling, made much of the sort of people he wanted to stay away, thank you very much. (Wordsworth got his come-uppance when one of the readers of his guide enjoyed it so much that he asked if he'd written anything else.) Good guides also need some of the robust challenge of Harriet Martineau's *Complete Guide to the Lakes*, published in 1855, which was the first fell walking guide for the common man. Indeed it's possible to argue that she invented fell walking as pastime – albeit a pastime that should be engaged in only after you'd hired the services of an experienced guide.

W. G. Collingwood, in his fine 1902 guidebook *The Lake Counties*, quotes a passage from Ruskin that captures how important it is to set landscape in context. Ruskin was describing a walking tour in the Alps, as it happens, but it could apply to his beloved Coniston Fells just as well. He was walking among flowers on the edge of a cliff overlooking a deep limestone valley cut through by a sparkling river. A hawk soared in the thermals. And he began to imagine he was in a previously undiscovered continent, devoid of history and romantic associations. And the landscape changed before his eyes:

> A sudden blankness and chill were cast upon it; the flowers in an instant lost their light, the river its music; the hills became oppressively desolate; a heaviness in the boughs of the darkened forest showed how much of their former power had been dependent on a life which was not theirs; how much of the glory of the imperishable or continually renewed creation is reflected from things more precious in their memories than in its renewing.

What he was experiencing is what any fell walker with a flicker of imagination or a morsel of soul has experienced in the hills – that scenery alone is not enough and that story alone is not enough. The alchemy of the mountains comes from the rocky crucible in which scenery and story are combined, hopefully with a handful of poetry and a sprinkling of romance.

Which, naturally enough, brings us to Alfred Wainwright. Naturally, because one of the secrets of his success is that he knew how to stir the crucible better than anyone of his generation.

Born in back-street Blackburn in 1907, he was an

unlikely champion of the mountains. His early life was dogged by poverty and uncertainty. His father, an itinerant stonemason, took to the drink and the young Alfred cast himself in the role of man of the house. In those days he didn't have time for ideas of adventure or excitement. His thoughts were focused on making something of himself so that he could provide for his mother. As he wrote in *Ex-Fellwanderer*: 'I wished I was old enough to go to work to help my mother, or find a buried treasure. But there were no buried treasures in Blackburn in those days and none above ground either.'

It would be more than twenty years before AW first saw the treasures buried in the Lakeland hills. In the meantime, at the age of thirteen, he applied for and got an office boy's job at Blackburn town hall. He ran all the way home to tell his mother that he was going to get fifteen bob a week. The pressure was off. Three years later he transferred to the borough treasurer's office and the start of a career among the immaculately kept ledgers that would be the second most important books in his life. The ledgers would eventually take him to a job in Kendal which offered him escape into the Lakeland mountains in every spare moment of his life.

But he first came to the Lake District in 1930. He couldn't get anyone from the office to come with him and he wasn't confident enough to make the trip alone, so he 'recruited' his cousin, Eric Beardsall, as travelling companion. By all accounts Eric was underwhelmed by the experience. He went to sleep in the grass on their first summit, Orrest Head. But AW was transfixed by the skyline of mountains. Here was Moses on Mount Pisgah having his sight of the promised land, Wordsworth on Snowdon and Ruskin and Coleridge in the Alps, all rolled into one. It was the moment when the temporal and eternal, the human and the divine, collided. It was a bolt of lightning that would illuminate more than fifty years of Wainwright's life.

The masterwork that was inspired by that first, visionary experience on Orrest Head was Wainwright's seven-volume Pictorial Guides to the Lakeland Fells. On 9 November 1952 Wainwright dipped pen into Indian ink and began drawing page one of Book One. He worked away at it for eight months and had completed more than a hundred pages when, as Hunter Davies says in his biography of Wainwright, he scrapped the lot and started again. The reason was that, although he'd aligned the left-hand side of every line of handwritten script, he hadn't aligned the right. He thought it looked scruffy. It wasn't the perfection for which he strived.

In the introduction to that very first Pictorial Guide, Wainwright gives us an example of the beguiling mixture of description and emotion, romance and memory, that would set his books on a shelf of their own in the huge library of Lakeland guides:

> Here, in small space, is the wonderland of childhood's dreams, lingering far beyond childhood through the span of a man's life .... How many, these memories .... the moment of wakening, and the sudden joyful realisation that this is to be another day of freedom on the hills .... the silence of lonely hills .... storm and tempest in the high places, and the unexpected glimpses of valleys dappled in sunlight far

beneath the swirling clouds .... rain, and the intimate shelter of lichened walls .... a sheepdog watching its master .... the snow and ice and freezing stillnesses of midwinter: a white world, rosy-pink as the sun goes down .... curling smoke from the chimneys of the farm down below amongst the trees, where the day shall end .... oil-lamps in flagged kitchens, huge fires in huge fireplaces, huge suppers .... glittering moonlight on placid waters .... stars above dark peaks .... the tranquillity that comes before sleep, when thoughts are of the day that is gone and the day that is to come .... All these memories, and so many more, breathing anew the rare quality and magical atmosphere of Lakeland .... memories that belong to Lakeland, and could not belong in the same way to any other place .... memories that enslave the mind forever.

Many are they who have fallen under the spell of Lakeland and many are they who have been moved to tell of their affection, in story and verse and picture and song.

This book is one man's way of expressing his devotion to Lakeland's friendly hills. It was conceived and is born after many years of inarticulate worshipping at their shrines. It is, in very truth, a love-letter.

Oh, to be as inarticulate.

And these are just the nursery slopes of an expedition into the high mountains in AW's company that will mix history and community, politics and philosophy, with the necessary practicalities of getting to the summit by every conceivable route. And on the way we'll be treated to the author's acerbic dislikes, elegant complaints and obsessive attention to detail. His passion for solitude; his hatred of overweening bureaucracy. His admiration for the fell shepherds; his contempt for tree-planting, reservoir-building vandals. All encapsulated in little works of superlative craftsmanship. Hand-drawn and hand-written to make sure that no slovenly mistakes could creep in during the production process.

When I was making the BBC television series with Wainwright, we often talked about the inspirations for the Pictorial Guides. He started off by maintaining that they were never intended for publication, that they were just a personal *aide memoire* which he'd be able to use as a work of reference when he became too decrepit to make it onto the hill – a personal memory of long-ago expeditions into paradise. I told him at the time that I didn't believe him – that they were obviously aimed at a wider audience. He humphed a bit and refused to talk about it for a day or two. But eventually he owned up. Yes, the first volume had started life as a scrapbook, but by the time he'd finished it he knew it was more, much more, than that. He was proud of it. Like all writers, he wanted to share his work and his ideas. He may well have liked to be alone on the hill but he loved the idea of having a million readers. Just so long as he didn't have to meet them or make conversation with them.

Which brings us, by a circuitous route through the hills, back to the subject of podcasts. I can imagine that there may be the odd Wainwright purist who wonders what AW would have made of this new technology. Obviously he'd be fuming, brewing up a storm on

Haystacks, where his ashes were scattered in 1991. After all, wasn't he the technophobe who couldn't bring himself to come to terms with computers, who didn't drive, who couldn't even change a light bulb? Well, yes, he was, but only because he had people to do that sort of thing for him. He managed to get through a whole, satisfying working life in pen and ink. He managed to get to most of the mountains by Ribble bus. And then he met Betty. He used to joke that he married his chauffeur. And if he pretended not to be able to change a light bulb, somebody else would do it and leave him to get on with the important things, such as writing his books. He had a charmed life.

Yes, he grumbled about the horrors of meeting up with noisy school parties on the hill but he also cared about getting his message from the mountains across to new generations of hill walkers. When my kids used to come out with me on filming days he would talk to them about how important it was to treat the hills with respect. Making the television programmes we worked on together may, at times, have seemed to him like supping with the devil, but he knew they were a way of getting an important message to a wider audience.

In the same way as he played to his (wholly inaccurate) image as the curmudgeonly old duffer, he led people to believe that he was a refugee from the eighteenth century. But he was much more modern than that. He espoused ideas of sustainability long before they were embraced by the chattering environmental classes. Thirty years ago he was addressing issues of landscape management which politicians are still failing to grasp.

I'm sure the podcasts wouldn't bother him one jot. If they brought just one visitor to a better understanding of his beloved Lake District, they'd be worth it.

Wainwright wouldn't be rushing to buy an iPod or an MP3 player himself, you understand. That would be expecting too much. But he would be encouraged by one thing. If somebody is listening to a podcast through earphones, at least they won't be talking on the hill. And in Wainwright's book – in all his books – that's the worst sin of all.

1 Catbells
from Hawse End

Geologically it's a mass of sheared and folded mud-
stone, siltstone and sandstone, which doesn't make
it sound very attractive. More poetically it's the
haven of the wild cat. Touristically it's the mountain
that visitors to Keswick see from Friar's Crag on
Derwent Water and say: 'We must go up there
tomorrow.' They go in their thousands, making
Catbells probably one of the most travelled bits of
high ground anywhere in Britain.

But that doesn't make it a bad mountain. It cast a
spell on Wainwright as it had cast a spell on many
Lakeland writers before him. John Ruskin said that the
view of it from Friar's Crag made Keswick almost too
beautiful a place to live in.

The author Hugh Walpole got closer still. He lived
at Brackenburn on the shoulder of Catbells, high
above Derwent Water, and in an essay published in
1934 described the view from it:

> There was the Lake more perfectly cupped than I had
> ever seen it from any other angle, Blencathra and
> Skiddaw hanging over Keswick, the town in the
> autumn haze like a skein of smokey wool; the
> mountains were in colour shell-rose but their 'tops'
> sharp as needles against the milky violet sky.

AW describes the same area, in his Personal Notes
in Conclusion at the end of *The North Western Fells*;
his description is more practical but still bursting
with the same fondness.

... the walking is quite excellent. The hills are easier to climb than their abrupt appearance suggests: the secret is to get on the ridges early, because it is the ridges, not the fellsides, that provide the best travelling underfoot and the finest views, and give the area its special appeal.

Wainwright spent two years exploring the north western fells, and during that time Catbells got to be rather like an old friend, the viewpoint equivalent of the well broken-in walking boot or the old sweater with just the right number of tobacco burns. He was supremely comfortable in its presence even though, many a day, he was just striding across it on the way to somewhere else.

In the years we were filming together, I noticed that he had a very particular way of communicating with mountains. An inclination of the head; a nod as if agreeing with some remark heard only by him; a smile as if sharing an arcane joke; a long sigh which could only mean that whatever the mountain may have said, Wainwright agreed with the point entirely.

So I'm imagining him on the ridge of Catbells, looking away towards Hindscarth and Robinson. Because I'm imagining the scene, they can both have a perfect sprinkling of snow, as in his illustration of them in the book. And then he walks a few paces and looks down into the charmed valley of Newlands. For a few moments he turns to the north west and Lord's Seat and Barf and Bassenthwaite (I wish he'd lived to see the ospreys back there). But then he sets his face to the south-west and the long rise out to Maiden

Moor and Dale Head beyond. There's the nod of the head and the smile and the sigh, and you just know that they're welcoming him back to days of wonderful adventures in the hills.

Descents
If you don't want to go down the same way that you came up, you have several alternatives. You can continue south, over the summit, down to Hause Gate, and there turn left and descend to Manesty, turning left again along either the old or the new road back to Hawse End, as detailed on Catbells page 6, and on the map on page 4. Or you can catch the launch back from Brandelhow. Or you can turn right at Hause Gate and return via Little Town, which appears in *The Tale of Mrs Tiggy-Winkle* by Beatrix Potter (see page 7).

Practical bits

Getting there
Hawse End is reached via the minor road along the western shore of Derwent Water: take the Portinscale turn off from the A66, continue south for about a mile and a half and at a fork take the left-hand road, signed for Grange.

Parking
There is a small car park near the cattle grid in the road. But given that parking here is very limited, a better way to start the walk is to combine it with a ride across Derwent Water. Leave the car in Keswick at the car park on Lake Road or one of the facilities in the

middle of the town, and take the ferry to Hawse End (see below).

Public transport
The Keswick Launch Company runs between three and ten services a day depending on the season (check times in advance by ringing 017687 72263 or online at www.keswick-launch.co.uk), and you are on the path up Catbells almost as on as you step off the boat.

The 77 Honister Rambler bus service runs between Keswick and Hawse End four times a day in each direction, daily between mid March and October, and on weekends in November. By boat or by bus, the journey takes about ten minutes. (See the Latrigg chapter for information about buses to and from Keswick.)

General
The nearest source of refreshments is the Swinside Inn, about half a mile from Hawse End. Portinscale has a hotel and café. Keswick has many more food options, plus a supermarket and smaller shops for putting together a picnic.

Catbells 1481'

Cat Bells
(two words)
on Ordnance maps

from Derwent Water

- Portinscale
  - Keswick

- Stair

▲ CATBELLS
- Little Town
▲ MAIDEN MOOR
  - Grange

MILES
0   1   2   3   4

from the Portinscale path

NATURAL FEATURES

Catbells is one of the great favourites, a family fell where grandmothers and infants can climb the heights together, a place beloved. Its popularity is well deserved: its shapely topknot attracts the eye, offering a steep but obviously simple scramble to the small summit; its slopes are smooth, sunny and sleek; its position overlooking Derwent Water is superb. Moreover, for stronger walkers it is the first step on a glorious ridge that bounds Borrowdale on the west throughout its length with Newlands down on the other side. There is beauty everywhere — and nothing but beauty. Its ascent from Keswick may conveniently, in the holiday season, be coupled with a sail on the lake, making the expedition rewarding out of all proportion to the small effort needed. Even the name has a magic challenge.

Yet this fell is not quite so innocuous as is usually thought, and grandmothers and infants should have a care as they romp around. There are some natural hazards in the form of a line of crags that starts at the summit and slants down to Newlands, and steep outcrops elsewhere. More dangerous are the levels and open shafts that pierce the fell on both flanks: the once-prosperous Yewthwaite Mine despoils a wide area in the combe above Little Town in Newlands, to the east the debris of the ill-starred Brandley Mine is lapped by the water of the lake, and the workings of the Old Brandley Mine, high on the side of the fell at Skelgill Bank, are in view on the ascent of the ridge from the north. A tragic death in one of the open Yewthwaite shafts in 1962 serves as a warning.

Words cannot adequately describe the rare charm of Catbells, nor its ravishing view. But no publicity is necessary: its mere presence in the Derwent Water scene is enough. It has a bold 'come hither' look that compels one's steps, and no suitor ever returns disappointed, but only looking back often. It has only to be seen from Friar's Crag — and a spell is cast. No Keswick holiday is consummated without a visit to Catbells.

from Yewthwaite Combe

Catbells 3

Crags and
Caverns
of Catbells

left : The crags of
Mart Bield,
below the summit
on the Newlands
side of the fell

right : A dangerous hole at
Yewthwaite Mine.
At the end of a rock cutting the
adit suggests a level (horizontal
tunnel) but in fact is the opening
of a vertical shaft.

below : Workings at the
Old Brandley Mine.
A shaft with twin entrances,
overhung by a tree, *left,* and
a nearby level, *right.*

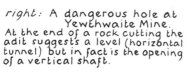
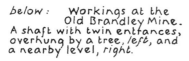

MAP

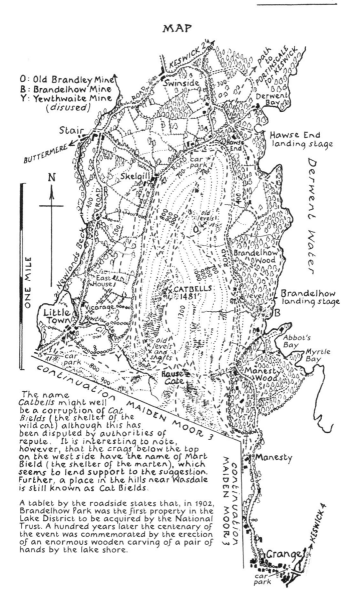

O : Old Brandley Mine
B : Brandelhow Mine
Y : Yewthwaite Mine
   (disused)

KESWICK 2¼

path to PORTINSCALE for KESWICK

Swinside

Derwent Bay

Stair

BUTTERMERE

Hawse End

Hawse End landing stage

car park

Skelgill

Derwent Water

N

ONE MILE

Newlands Beck

East House

Vicarage

Little Town

Yewthwaite Gill

car park

Brandelhow Wood

CATBELLS 1481

old levels

Brandelhow landing stage

B

Abbot's Bay

Myrtle Bay

old levels X shafts

Hause Gate

Manesty Wood

continuation MAIDEN MOOR 3

Manesty

continuation MAIDEN MOOR 3

Grange

KESWICK 4

car park

The name *Catbells* might well be a corruption of *Cat Bields* (the shelter of the wild cat) although this has been disputed by authorities of repute. It is interesting to note, however, that the crags below the top on the west side have the name of *Mart Bield* (the shelter of the marten), which seems to lend support to the suggestion. Further, a place in the hills near Wasdale is still known as *Cat Bields*.

A tablet by the roadside states that, in 1902, Brandelhow Park was the first property in the Lake District to be acquired by the National Trust. A hundred years later the centenary of the event was commemorated by the erection of an enormous wooden carving of a pair of hands by the lake shore.

ASCENT FROM HAWSE END
1250 feet of ascent : 1½ miles

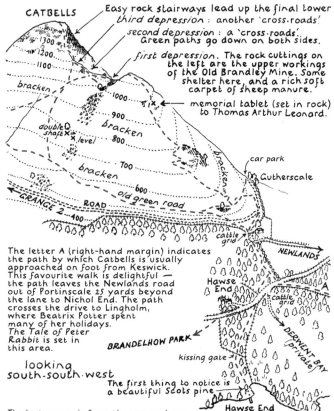

CATBELLS

Easy rock stairways lead up the final tower
third depression : another 'cross-roads'

second depression : a 'cross-roads'.
Green paths go down on both sides.

first depression. The rock cuttings on
the left are the upper workings
of the Old Brandley Mine. Some
shelter here, and a rich soft
carpet of sheep manure.

1300
1200
1100

bracken

1000

900

bracken

double
shaft
level

800

700

bracken

600

old green road

GRANGE 2

ROAD

400

— memorial tablet (set in rock)
to Thomas Arthur Leonard.

car park

Gutherscale

cattle
grid

NEWLANDS

Hawse
End

cattle
grid

A

BRANDELHOW PARK

kissing gate

DERWENT BAY (private)

looking
south·south·west

The first thing to notice is
a beautiful Scots pine

Hawse End
landing stage

Derwent Water

The letter A (right-hand margin) indicates
the path by which Catbells is usually
approached on foot from Keswick.
This favourite walk is delightful —
the path leaves the Newlands road
out of Portinscale 25 yards beyond
the lane to Nichol End. The path
crosses the drive to Lingholm,
where Beatrix Potter spent
many of her holidays.
The Tale of Peter
Rabbit is set in
this area.

The best way up is from the car park on
the Skelgill road. It is paved and gently
graded throughout. For those who arrive
by bus or on foot an alternative path
leaves from the road junction and curves
left to join the path from the car park.

Woodford's Path:
 This series of zigzags was engineered
by Sir John Woodford, who lived near,
and his name deserves to be remembered
by those who use his enchanting stairway.
It starts 80 yards along the old green road.

Hawse End is served
by motor·launch from
Keswick.

One of the very best
of the shorter climbs.
A truly lovely walk.

ASCENT FROM GRANGE
1250 feet of ascent : 2 miles

Of course there is no gate at Hause Gate, just as there is no door at Mickledoor. 'Gate' and 'door' are local geographical terms for a way or opening through the hills or across a ridge. 'Hause' is another good Lakeland name for a pass. 'Hause Gate' is therefore really a tautological name. 'Hawse End' (with a 'w') is not a mis-spelling, 'hause' being inappropriate to the place.

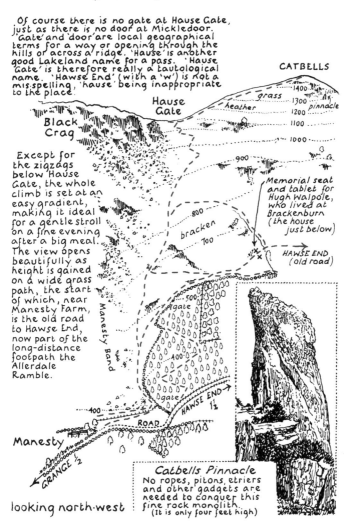

CATBELLS

Hause Gate

grass

heather

1400

1300 — pinnacle

1200

1100

1000

Black Crag

900

Memorial seat and tablet for Hugh Walpole, who lived at Brackenburn (the house just below)

Except for the zigzags below Hause Gate, the whole climb is set at an easy gradient, making it ideal for a gentle stroll on a fine evening after a big meal. The view opens beautifully as height is gained on a wide grass path, the start of which, near Manesty Farm, is the old road to Hawse End, now part of the long-distance footpath the Allerdale Ramble.

800

bracken

700

HAWSE END (old road)

Manesty Band

500

gate

400

gate

HAWSE END 1½

400

Manesty

ROAD

GRANGE ½

looking north-west

Catbells Pinnacle
No ropes, pitons, etriers and other gadgets are needed to conquer this fine rock monolith.
(It is only four feet high)

ASCENT FROM NEWLANDS

via SKELGILL
1200 feet of ascent: 1½ miles from Stair

via LITTLE TOWN
950 feet of ascent: 1¾ miles from Little Town

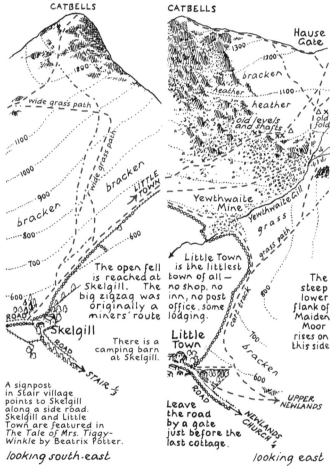

CATBELLS

1200

wide grass path

wide grass path

bracken

LITTLE TOWN

1100

1000

900

bracken

800

600

700

600

ROAD

Skelgill

ROAD

STAIR ½

The open fell is reached at Skelgill. The big zigzag was originally a miners' route

There is a camping barn at Skelgill.

A signpost in Stair village points to Skelgill along a side road. Skelgill and Little Town are featured in *The Tale of Mrs. Tiggy-Winkle* by Beatrix Potter.

looking south-east

CATBELLS

Hause Gate

1300   1200

bracken

heather   1100

heather

old levels and shafts

old fold

Yewthwaite Mine

Yewthwaite Gill

grass

grass path

Little Town is the littlest town of all — no shop, no inn, no post office, some lodging.

cart track

600

700

600

Little Town

bracken

ROAD

NEWLANDS CHURCH

UPPER NEWLANDS

The steep lower flank of Maiden Moor rises on this side

Leave the road by a gate just before the last cottage.

looking east

Up one way and down the other is a nice idea

THE SUMMIT

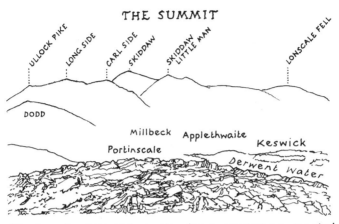

The summit, which has no cairn, is a small platform of naked rock, light brown in colour and seamed and pitted with many tiny hollows and crevices that collect and hold rainwater — so that, long after the skies have cleared, glittering diamonds adorn the crown. Almost all the native vegetation has been scoured away by the varied footgear of countless visitors; so popular is this fine viewpoint that often it is difficult to find a vacant perch. In summer this is not a place to seek quietness.
DESCENTS: Leave the top only by the ridge; lower down there is a wealth of choice. Keep clear of the craggy Newlands face.

RIDGE ROUTE

To MAIDEN MOOR, 1887'
1½ miles : S, then SW
Depression (Hause Gate) at 1180'
720 feet of ascent

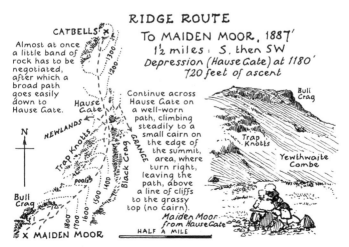

Almost at once a little band of rock has to be negotiated, after which a broad path goes easily down to Hause Gate.

Continue across Hause Gate on a well-worn path, climbing steadily to a small cairn on the edge of the summit area, where turn right, leaving the path, above a line of cliffs to the grassy top (no cairn).

Maiden Moor from Hause Gate
HALF A MILE

THE VIEW

Scenes of great beauty unfold on all sides, and they are scenes in depth to a degree not usual, the narrow summit permitting downward views of Borrowdale and Newlands within a few paces. Nearby valley and lake attract the eye more than the distant mountain surround, although Hindscarth and Robinson are particularly prominent at the head of Newlands and Causey Pike towers up almost grotesquely directly opposite. On this side the hamlet of Little Town is well seen down below, a charming picture, but it is to Derwent Water and mid-Borrowdale that the captivated gaze returns again and again.

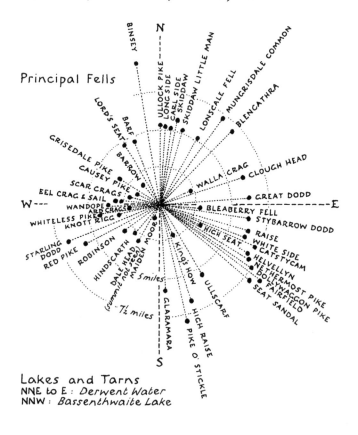

Principal Fells

Lakes and Tarns
NNE to E : Derwent Water
NNW : Bassenthwaite Lake

Hindscarth and Robinson from Catbells

2 Coniston Old Man
from Coniston

I rarely disagreed with Wainwright, but when it came to Coniston Old Man I made an exception. He described it as a devastated place, scarred and disfigured, a mountain licking its wounds. Well, five hundred years of quarrying and mining have certainly left their mark in the spoil heaps and tunnels and clefts that crowd in along Coppermines Valley. But I find it a fascinating place. In the same way that Wainwright could hear the whispers of the mountains, on the ascent of Coniston Old Man I get a sense of the people who worked there for all those years. On tracks where we walk for pleasure and diversion would once have tramped men on their way to a long shift underground. Stop by the chasms that connect with the underground workings and I defy you not to imagine the sound of hammer on rock and the creak of rope and winch. It's that sort of place.

A few years ago I was filming at Levers Water, under Coniston Old Man. For years it was used as a reservoir to feed water wheels in the mine workings down the valley. On the way up I'd been talking to the film crew about sensing the spirit of the miners that seemed to be imprinted on the valley. They, of course, said they thought I was talking nonsense. Film crews are like that. Any mention of culture, poetry or spirits (other than a large Jack Daniels after a hard day's filming) and they tend to glaze over. Anyhow, they set up the camera just below the reservoir dam. I was going to walk across through the inch or so of water that was flowing over the rocky lip out of Levers Water. Jan, the cameraman, said the camera was running and that I should watch out for the spirits of dead miners. I walked across and just as I got to the other side a mini tornado spiralled across the surface of the lake, picking up water as it went which it proceeded to dump on the crew. Make of that what you will.

Anyhow, you're safe because Levers Water is a diversion from your route, You're travelling via the rather less spirited Low Water. And this is where AW and I start to agree again. He says Low Water is the perfect place to lie back and take a break, and nobody could possibly disagree with that. Nor could anyone quibble with the fact that once you've made it to the summit you've reached one of the very best viewing platforms in the whole of Lakeland. And one of the best views from it is the bird's eye view of the way you've just come – the zig-zag track up from Low Water.

The view is made, for me, by the glittering seascapes to the south, which provide a glorious counterpoint to the mountains crowding away to the north. There's an array of summits stretching as far as Skiddaw – 19 miles away by AW's reckoning. And east–west too, stretching from Harter Fell to Harter Fell: Harter by Kentmere Pike in the east, and Harter above Eskdale in the west. That's a crossing of Lakeland that I intend to do one day. But it would make a very long podcast.

Descents
If you don't want to go down the same way that you came up, the best route down is via Goat's Water and

the Walna Scar road. (See Coniston Old Man page 9 for details and pages 5–6 for a map.)

Practical bits

Parking
Coniston's most convenient car park is the one run by the National Park Authority. It's in the centre of the village by the Tourist Information Centre and is clearly signed off the B5285 as you drive through. There's more parking by the lake, which is handy if you're planning a visit there too.

Public transport
Coniston isn't very well served by public transport, although the 505 Coniston Rambler bus service links it with Windermere, Ambleside and Hawkshead daily between mid March and early November. From the west, the X12 will get you there from Ulverston every day except Sundays.

General
There are several pubs and cafés to choose from in Coniston, plus plenty of small shops from which you could put together a decent picnic – plus all the outdoor clothing and equipment stores you could ever wish for.

Coniston Old Man

2633'

properly
The Old Man of Coniston

from Red Dell Head

NATURAL FEATURES

The Coniston fells form a separate geographical unit. They are almost entirely severed from the adjacent mountainous parts of Lakeland by the Duddon and Brathay valleys, with the watershed between the two, Wrynose Pass, 1270', providing the only link with other fells. Before 1974 all the Coniston fells were within Lancashire, the two valleys mentioned containing the boundaries of Cumberland (Duddon) and Westmorland (Brathay). Now the whole of the Lake District is in Cumbria.

Whilst the characteristics of the Coniston fells are predominantly Lakeland, with lofty ridges, steep and craggy declivities, lovely waterfalls and lonely tarns and the general scenic charm so typical of the district, there has been a great deal of industrial exploitation here, principally in copper mining (now abandoned) and quarrying (still active), resulting in much disfigurement. So strongly sculptured are these fine hills, however, and so pronounced is their appeal that the scars detract but little from the attractiveness of the picture : many people, indeed, will find that the decayed skeletons of the mine-workings add an unusual interest to their walks.

The western slopes are comparatively dull, and the appeal of these hills lies in their aspect to the east, where the village of Coniston, in an Alpine setting, is the natural base for explorations. The ridge-walking, on soft turf, is excellent, but all slopes are very rough down to valley-level. As viewpoints, the summits have the advantage of isolation between the main mass of Lakeland and the fine indented coastline of Morecambe Bay, the prospects in all directions being of a high quality.

Waterfalls
Church Beck

continued

NATURAL FEATURES

continued

The pattern of the Coniston Fells

Wrynose Pass → Brathay

Greenburn Res.ʳ (disused)

Duddon

Land over 1500':
- over 2500'
- 2000'-2500'
- 1500'-2000'

Levers Water

Seathwaite Tarn

Low Water

Coniston

1: THE OLD MAN
2: SWIRL HOW
3: BRIM FELL
4: GREAT CARRS
5: DOW CRAG
6: GREY FRIAR
7: WETHERLAM

Goat's Water

Walna Scar Pass

N

The northern Coniston Fells from Little Langdale

Wrynose Pass

NATURAL FEATURES

The highest (by a few feet) and best-known of the Coniston fells is the Old Man, a benevolent giant revered by generations of walkers and of particular esteem in the eyes of the inhabitants of the village he shelters, for he has contributed much to their prosperity. The Old Man is no Matterhorn, nor is Coniston a Zermatt, but an affinity is there in the same close links between mountain and village, and the history of the one is the history of the other. Coniston without its Old Man is unthinkable.

Yet the Old Man has little significance in the geographical arrangements hereabouts, the true hub of this group of hills being Swirl How, a summit of slightly lower elevation northwards. The Old Man is merely the termination of Swirl How's main ridge and ends high Lakeland in the south: the last outpost, looking far over the sea.

Although cruelly scarred and mutilated by quarries the Old Man has retained a dignified bearing, and still raises his proud and venerable head to the sky. His tears are shed quietly into Low Water and Goat's Water, two splendid tarns, whence, in due course, and after further service to the community in the matter of supplies of electricity and water, they ultimately find their way into Coniston's lake, and there bathe his ancient feet.

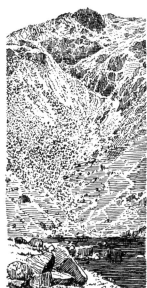

The Old Man from Low Water

Yet even during these peaceful ablutions the Old Man continues to be harassed. On the day this page was first prepared (November 10th 1958) the world's water speed record was broken on Coniston Water, by Donald Campbell. Thus, from tip to toe, the mountain serves man. *POSTSCRIPT*: In 1967 Donald Campbell died on Coniston Water attempting to break the record again.

MAP

MAP

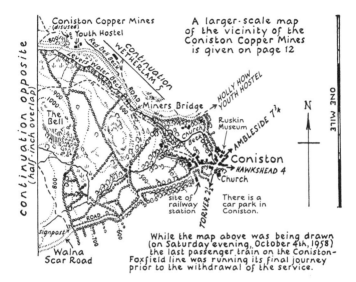

A larger-scale map of the vicinity of the Coniston Copper Mines is given on page 12

Coniston Copper Mines (disused)
Youth Hostel
continuation WETHERLAMS
Levers Water Beck
Red Dell Beck
ROAD
continuation opposite (half-inch overlap)
The Bell
800
1,000
Miners Bridge
HOLLY HOW YOUTH HOSTEL
AMBLESIDE 7¾
Ruskin Museum
church beck
Coniston
HAWKSHEAD 4
Church
ONE MILE
N
site of railway station
TORVER 2½
There is a car park in Coniston.
ROAD
700
signpost
Walna Scar Road

While the map above was being drawn (on Saturday evening, October 4th, 1958) the last passenger train on the Coniston-Foxfield line was running its final journey prior to the withdrawal of the service.

Detail is not given of the territory south of the Walna Scar Road except in the vicinity of the approach from Torver. Here is little to tempt the fellwalker, for a broad and dreary moor declines to the cultivated shores of Coniston Water, but this rather desolate expanse nevertheless is fruitful ground for the antiquary, there being many evidences of a civilisation long past. Ancient cairns, walled enclosures and stone circles are all revealed to the eager and learned searcher amongst the bracken, and excavators have unearthed a Bronze Age cemetery. How odd that the scene of these mouldering relics should be also the place where an ultra-modern flying saucer was first photographed!

Somewhere in the area covered by the map on the opposite page, *but not indicated*, is a small upright memorial stone roughly inscribed 'CHARMER 1911'. Charmer was a foxhound killed in a fall on Dow Crag, and it is rather nice to know that the memory of a faithful dog was revered in this way. But some visitors have seen nothing sacred in the stone and it has been uprooted and cast aside on occasion. For this reason it has been thought best not to disclose its exact location. Rest in peace, Charmer. They were happy days.........

Charmer's Grave

ASCENT FROM CONISTON (via BOO TARN)

2400 feet of ascent: 3 miles

CONISTON OLD MAN

south ridge

looking north-west

2100

old quarries

grass

2000

1900

old quarries

1800

1700

pool

Bursting Stone Quarry

1600

1500

spoil heap

1400

1300

1400

1200

1300

1200

quarry road

Timley Knott

1100

1000

WALNA SCAR 2

bracken

900

Braidy Beck

Boo Tarn (a small reedy pool)

dried-up tarn

bracken

800

old quarry road

gate

CONISTON ¾

signpost

An old cave at Bursting Stone Quarry (now gone)

The signpost points along the old quarry road to the Old Man, but take the Walna Scar path.

Just as the first edition of this book went to press, in 1960, there was news that Bursting Stone Quarry was soon to be reopened. It is still operating today (2006), having in the meantime played havoc with the route the author described on this page. The route starts promisingly in the vicinity of Boo Tarn with a clear path and a sign saying 'Footpath to the Old Man', but in a quarter of a mile the path peters out. When this happens, aim for the top of the prominent spoil heap on the right. Then follow the higher of the two disused quarry roads. It heads up to the left at first and then doubles back to the right. After passing a pool strike up the hill following a single-strand fence. When the fence reaches its highest point look for a very faint path on the left. This eventually joins the main path to the Old Man from the east.

ASCENT FROM CONISTON (DIRECT)
2450 feet of ascent : 3 miles (2½ via Church Beck)

looking west

CONISTON OLD MAN

This is the way the crowds go: the day trippers, the courting couples, troops of earnest Boy Scouts, babies and grandmothers, the lot. On this stony parade fancy handbags and painted toenails are as likely to be seen as rucksacks and boots. In its favour, it can be said that the route is absolutely safe in the worst weather — the densest mist cannot obscure the spiralling ribbon of stones. But let's be fair — the scenery of Low Water is very good.

south ridge

BRIM FELL

2500
2400
2300
2200
2100
2000
1900

spoil

cave (shelter)

Low Water — a good place for giving up and going to sleep.

main quarry

1700

old water pipe

spoil heaps

tunnel
1600

ruin containing old mining machinery

1500
× × ruins

Colt Crag

1300

1200

5 minutes level walk to the giant Pudding Stone

-1200

1100

BOULDER VALLEY

grass path

900

1000

old quarry road

800

WALNA SCAR

signpost

car park

gate

bracken

800

juniper

700

LEVERS WATER BECK

800

YOUTH HOSTEL

700

600

Aspiring ascenders of the Old Man are directed by signposts to take the Walna Scar road and then the old quarry road, but some relief from stones underfoot may be gained initially by using the much pleasanter route via Church Beck. (Turn right behind the Sun Hotel.)

Miners Bridge
waterfall

Church Beck

CONISTON

Meanwhile the discerning walker is enjoying a solitary and undisturbed climb on the sweet grass above Boo Tarn. The page to which he refers is occasionally is Coniston Old Man 7 not 8.

500

400

300

signpost

200

Sun Hotel

BROUGHTON 9

Black Bull Hotel

Coniston (car park)

ASCENT FROM TORVER
2350 feet of ascent : 3¼ miles (3¾ via Goat's Hawse)

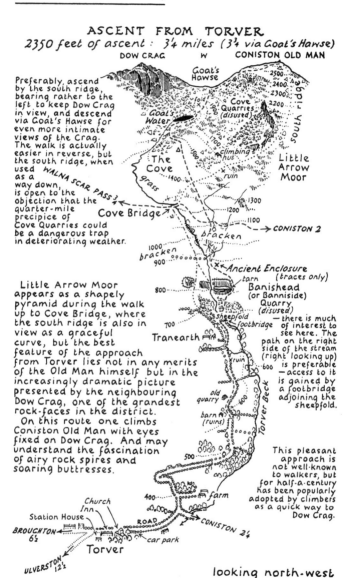

DOW CRAG   W   CONISTON OLD MAN

Goat's Hawse

2500
2400
2300
2200

South ridge

fold

900

Cove Quarries (disused)

Goat's Water

Preferably, ascend by the south ridge, bearing rather to the left to keep Dow Crag in view, and descend via Goat's Hawse for even more intimate views of the Crag. The walk is actually easier in reverse, but the south ridge, when used as a way down, is open to the objection that the quarter-mile precipice of Cove Quarries could be a dangerous trap in deteriorating weather.

WALNA SCAR PASS

climbing hut

Little Arrow Moor

The Cove

grass

1400

ruin

Cove Bridge

1300

1200

1100

→ CONISTON 2

bracken

1000 bracken
900

Ancient Enclosure (traces only)

tarn

Banishead (or Banniside) Quarry (disused)

800

— there is much of interest to see here. The path on the right side of the stream (right looking up) is preferable — access to it is gained by a footbridge adjoining the sheepfold.

Little Arrow Moor appears as a shapely pyramid during the walk up to Cove Bridge, where the south ridge is also in view as a graceful curve, but the best feature of the approach from Torver lies not in any merits of the Old Man himself but in the increasingly dramatic picture presented by the neighbouring Dow Crag, one of the grandest rock-faces in the district.
On this route one climbs Coniston Old Man with eyes fixed on Dow Crag. And may understand the fascination of airy rock spires and soaring buttresses.

700

sheepfold
footbridge

Tranearth

ruin

600

old quarry

barn (ruins)

500

Torver Beck

This pleasant approach is not well-known to walkers, but for half-a-century has been popularly adopted by climbers as a quick way to Dow Crag.

400

farm

Church Inn
Station House

ROAD

BROUGHTON 6½

car park

Torver

→ CONISTON 2¼

ULVERSTON 12½

looking north-west

*Boulder
Valley*

Low Water Beck falls in steep cascades from its tarn to a level shelf 600 feet below and there meanders uncertainly before resuming its hurried journey to join Levers Water Beck.

This shelf is littered with boulders tumbled from the craggy slopes above, a scene common enough among the mountains, but in this particular instance several of the boulders are of quite uncommon size, big enough indeed to provide some entertainment and practice for rock-climbers, who name the area Boulder Valley.

The most massive and most prominent of the boulders is the Pudding Stone, 25 feet high and as big as a house, which has a dozen climbing routes, one of them being considered easy, but not by everybody, and the others, by walkers' standards, ranging between various grades of impossibility. The Pudding Stone may not have the overall dimensions of the Bowder Stone in Borrowdale, but certainly gives the impression of a greater bulk and weight.

*The Pudding Stone
(the easy side)*

*It is perhaps
unnecessary
to add that the
figure up aloft
is not the author*

Coppermines Valley

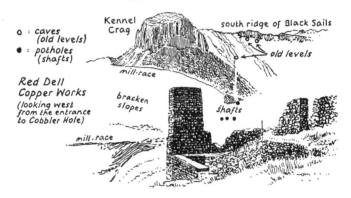

o : caves (old levels)

● : potholes (shafts)

Kennel Crag

south ridge of Black Sails

old levels

mill-race

Red Dell Copper Works (looking west from the entrance to Cobbler Hole)

bracken slopes

shafts

mill-race

Fellwalkers based on Coniston need not sit moping in their lodgings if a wet day puts the high tops out of bounds for it is possible to occupy the mind and keep the body reasonably dry by dodging from one to another of the many caves, levels and tunnels of the Coppermines Valley, one mile distant.

This hollow among the hills presents a surprising scene of squalid desolation, typical of the dreary outskirts of many coalmining towns but utterly foreign to the Lake District, and it says much for the quality of the encircling mountains that they can triumph over the serious disfigurement of ugly spoil heaps and gaping wounds, and still look majestic. Here, in this strange amphitheatre, where flowers once grew, one sees the hopeless debris of the ruins of workings long abandoned, where flowers will never grow again, and, as always in the presence of death, is saddened — but a raising of the eyes discloses a surround of noble heights, and then the heart is uplifted too.

There is good fun and absorbing interest in locating all the tunnels and shafts of the former quarries and mines. The shafts, hideous potholes falling sheer into black depths, have now been provided with protective fences, and most of the hazardous passages are no longer accessible, but there are exceptions, and passages should be entered only with great caution: we can't afford to lose any readers here, not with a further three volumes of the second edition still to be sold. A more detailed description of this area will be found in *Coniston Copper Mines: A Field Guide* by Eric G. Holland, published by the Cicerone Press in 1981 and reprinted with amendments in 2000. This includes details of passages that may be safely entered and eight-figure grid references for all entrances.

The accompanying map indicates the various holes of one sort and another in the Coppermines Valley area. There are others elsewhere on the Coniston fells, notably on Wetherlam.

continuing *Coppermines Valley*

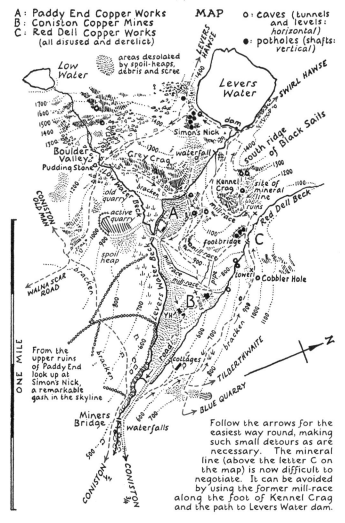

A: Paddy End Copper Works
B: Coniston Copper Mines
C: Red Dell Copper Works
(all disused and derelict)

MAP

o: caves (tunnels and levels: horizontal)
●: potholes (shafts: vertical)

areas desolated by spoil-heaps, debris and scree

Low Water

Levers Water

LEVERS HAWSE

SWIRL HAWSE

1700
1600
1500
1400
1300

dam

south ridge of Black Sails

Simon's Nick

Boulder Valley
Pudding Stone

Grey Crag

waterfall

1300
1200
1100

Kennel Crag

site of mineral line ruins

CONISTON OLD MAN

Low Water Beck

old quarry

bracken

1200

mill-race

Red Dell Beck

active quarry

A

1100

footbridge

C

mill-race

spoil heap

pipe

900

mill-race

level

Cobbler Hole

WALNA SCAR ROAD

bracken

Levers Water Beck

mill-race

800
700
600

B

YH

road

700

bracken

800
900
1000
1100

ONE MILE

From the upper ruins of Paddy End look up at Simon's Nick, a remarkable gash in the skyline

cottages

TILBERTHWAITE

BLUE QUARRY

Miners Bridge

waterfalls

500
600
700

CONISTON ½
CONISTON ¾

N

Follow the arrows for the easiest way round, making such small detours as are necessary. The mineral line (above the letter C on the map) is now difficult to negotiate. It can be avoided by using the former mill-race along the foot of Kennel Crag and the path to Levers Water dam.

THE SUMMIT

Tourists looking for Blackpool Tower

Boy Scouts

Typical summit scene

Solitary fellwalker, bless him, looking north to the hills

There may be a cairn on the summit, or there may not.........
Sometimes there is, sometimes there isn't......... The frequent
visitor gains the impression that a feud rages here between
cairn-builders and cairn-destroyers, with the contestants evenly
matched, so that one week there will be a cairn, the next week
not, and so on. Indestructible, however, is a big solidly-constructed
slate platform on which the cairn, when there is one, stands, and
which has no counterpart on other fells; into it a recess has been
provided and this serves as a shallow wind-shelter on occasions
when it is not cluttered up with the debris of shattered cairns, the
latter circumstance depending on which of the rival factions is, at
the moment, enjoying a temporary and fleeting triumph. One
hesitates to join in, if this is a private fight, but may perhaps suggest
that if the word 'man' means 'a summit cairn', as authorities seem
to be agreed, then, of all fells, the Old Man should be allowed to
have one and that it should be left alone to grow hoary and
ancient. But it never could. Not with those crowds.

An Ordnance Survey triangulation column stands on the
north side of the platform. A hundred yards south-east of
the summit is a low mound of stones which marks the start
of the steep descent to Coniston.

The summit is directly above
the very rough eastern slope,
which falls precipitously to
the black pool of Low Water;
in other directions gradients
are easy, predominantly with
a surface of grass but having
an occasional rash of stones.

In places where the native
rock crops out, weathering
has reduced it to vertical
flakes occurring in series.

Typical rock formations on the summit

THE SUMMIT

DESCENTS:

TO CONISTON:

Although the start of the usual quarries path is indistinct for a few yards as it leaves the summit there should be no difficulty in finding and following it, even in the thickest mist: the path is one of the safest and surest (and stoniest) in the district.

The Boo Tarn route leaves the quarries path indistinctly after two hundred yards and is marked by cairns. This route is difficult to follow up or down, and is confusing in mist. When you come to a single-strand fence follow it down to the right to a disused road that bends left and leads to Bursting Stone Quarry.

TO TORVER:

Follow the south ridge (no path) to hit the Walna Scar Road anywhere, after which it is easy going; but the lower slopes of the ridge are rough and thick with bracken and are best avoided by inclining to the right *after Cove Quarries are passed* to join the good path from Goat's Water near the ruins of Cove Hut. *The quarries are an ugly trap in mist.*

When the Walna Scar Road is reached carry straight on through a maze of paths to Banishead Quarry, passing it on the left. At the foot of the slag heaps cross over the footbridge, and join the lane that links the climbing hut at Tranearth with the village of Torver.

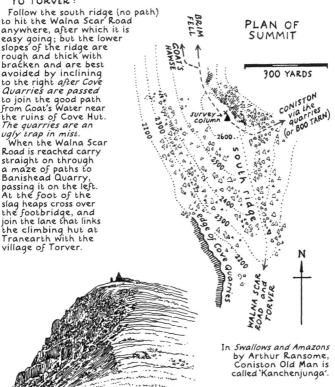

PLAN OF SUMMIT

300 YARDS

In *Swallows and Amazons* by Arthur Ransome, Coniston Old Man is called 'Kanchenjunga'.

The summit from the north

The Coniston Fells: looking north along the ridge from the Old Man

A note on the names of fells:

Newcomers to Lakeland may wonder why many names of fells are prominently inscribed on Ordnance Survey maps yet rarely find mention in guidebooks and other literature descriptive of the district. This neglect of official names can be explained by reference to the Coniston area as an example. Thus the compact group of hills known to walkers as the Coniston Fells is, according to the Ordnance Survey, more properly described as a part of the Furness Fells, and this latter title appears in widely-spaced capital letters on their 1″ maps. So far all right, but then this general name of the whole has several sub-titles in smaller but quite prominent letters for particular (but ill-defined) sections — Cockley Beck Fell, Seathwaite Fells, Tilberthwaite High Fells, Troutal Fell, Coniston Fells (an area east of the principal ridge), Above Beck Fells, and so on. These names mean little to the walker, who soon trains his eye, when looking at the map, to ignore them. His interest is in the names of the separate hills and summits.

Of course the Ordnance Survey is correct in using the local names of fells, which indicate not hills but indefinite areas of uncultivated high ground and other rough pastures: in general, sheep-grazing areas. Walkers are quite wrong in applying the name of a summit to the whole fell as they do. Wetherlam, for instance, is the name of the top of a fell only, the fell itself being named variously according to its different sections, e.g. Tilberthwaite High Fells, Low Fell, Above Beck Fells. These local distinctions are of no use to walkers, who want one name per hill, although, on occasion, in the absence of a name for a summit, one of them may be adopted, e.g. Brim Fell.

The ideal map for fellwalkers would omit detail of purely local interest (and parish and other boundaries), and name all summits distinctively. *Do one for us, O.S., please.*

RIDGE ROUTES

To BRIM FELL, 2611′ : ½ mile : N
Depression at 2545′ : 80 feet of ascent
   A ten minutes' stroll on excellent turf
Brim Fell is the rounded top next on
the ridge northwards.   In mist it
would be easy to take the Goat's
Hawse path by mistake, but not if
it is remembered that the route
keeps to the ridge all the way.

To DOW CRAG, 2555′ : 1 mile :
NW, W, SW and S
Depression (Goat's Hawse) at 2130′
   425 feet of ascent
   A walk of increasing interest
An expert rockclimber who is also a good swimmer might attempt a
straight course between the two summits, but ordinary mortals are
forced to make a considerable detour *via* Goat's Hawse. A good path
starts at the top of the Old Man and follows the ridge to the north.
Turn left at the first junction and follow the path down to Goat's Hawse.
After crossing the Hawse, a simple horizontal traverse may be made to
the base of the great crag for a close view of the rock buttresses,
but there is no trace of a path and the ground is extremely stony.

Dow Crag
 from the Old Man

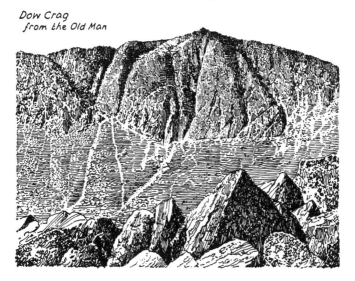

THE VIEW

A vast seascape makes a glorious sweep across the southern horizon, ranging from the Pennines to Black Combe, and, further west, to the Isle of Man. A rare beauty is added to the scene by the silver waters of the Kent, Leven and Duddon estuaries. Most people who climb the Old Man, not being fellwalkers, fix their eyes in this direction, and squeals of joy announce the sighting of Calder Hall Power Station, Blackpool Tower, Morecambe Battery, the monument on Ulverston's Hoad Hill, Millom and sundry other man-made monstrosities. This book does not deign to cater for such tastes.

The fellwalker will prefer to gaze across the gulf of Eskdale to the natural and unmarred grandeur of the Scafell group, but, this scene apart, the mountain panorama, although very extensive, is a little disappointing due to the intervening bulk of the other Coniston fells. The peep over the edge at the path zig-zagging upwards from Low Water, the tarn directly below, is, however, striking — the best bird's-eye view of an ascent-route in Lakeland.

Swirl How is a much better viewpoint for the man who would rather look at hills than at Millom, and moreover, the peace will not be disturbed by squealing women and children and by knowledgeable males who noisily identify wrongly every hill in sight. Before fleeing to this sanctuary, however, wander a little way down the western slope until out of earshot of the congregation on the summit and so come face to face with the magnificent front of Dow Crag — and agree that nature fashions the finest architecture whatever the folk on the top may say.

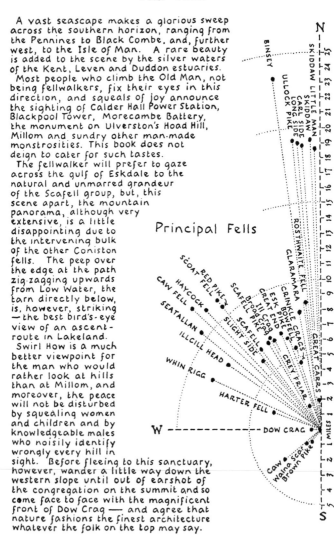

Principal Fells

THE VIEW

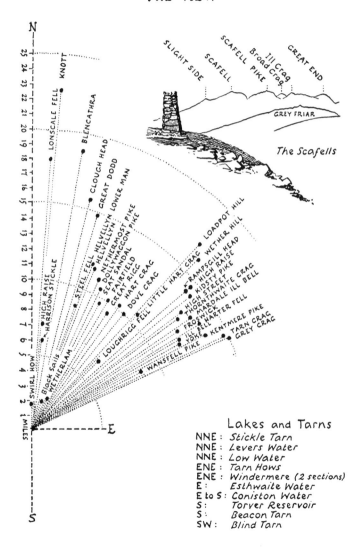

The Scafells

Lakes and Tarns

NNE : *Stickle Tarn*
NNE : *Levers Water*
NNE : *Low Water*
ENE : *Tarn Hows*
ENE : *Windermere (2 sections)*
E : *Esthwaite Water*
E to S : *Coniston Water*
S : *Torver Reservoir*
S : *Beacon Tarn*
SW : *Blind Tarn*

3 Haystacks
from Gatesgarth

Long before Wainwright's last, sad journey out onto Haystacks as a box of ashes, he'd paved the way for his arrival – done his best to ensure that the spirits of the mountain would have a welcome on the hillside prepared for him when the time came.

Apparently some unwary soul had been rash enough to suggest that Haystacks, at 1900 feet, didn't qualify as a mountain. It would need to be 2000 feet before it could even be considered. Wainwright's reaction was volcanic and made more impressive still by the plume of Three Nuns smoke that rose vertically from his pipe as if driven up by some set of embedded bellows. I expected magma to pour from the bowl at any moment.

'Haystacks would be mortally offended if classed merely as a hill. Everything expected of a mountain is here in full measure: rocks, crags, bogs, runnels of water, tarns, boulders, scree and glorious views.' That's the way he put it in *Wainwright's Favourite Lakeland Mountains.* He was even blunter the day he and I touched on the subject of Haystacks while standing outside the Black Sail Youth Hostel. We were waiting for a film crew to do the sort of technical things that film crews do and that are a mystery to human beings. And suddenly, up from the geological depths, rumbled the Wainwrightian broadside.

For a moment I thought he was about to swear, but he pulled himself back from the brink. Instead he gave a forensic analysis of THOSE PEOPLE who simply didn't understand mountains; who OBVIOUSLY had no soul.

Obviously.

Sensible people don't disagree with volcanoes.

Mountains were part of the Wainwright circle of family and friends. He cared about them. They were always in his thoughts. When he was apart from them, he was lonely. Every mountain exploration was a homecoming. When his eyesight began to fail and he had, eventually, to give up his adventures in the hills, in the mountain mists he sensed them weeping for him. And after Betty, and Totty, his cat, his dearest friend was Haystacks.

In one way, it was Wainwright who discovered Haystacks. Of course, it had always been there, in the shadow of Gable and Pillar, but early guidebook writers had tended to ignore it. A thousand feet smaller than its neighbours, its humps and hollows and little tarns, if mentioned at all, were mentioned in passing, on the way to somewhere more interesting.

But on his way to creating the Haystacks fan club Wainwright spent days and weeks exploring its tumbled, jumbled summit. He spent hours sitting by Innominate Tarn. He photographed it, he drew it, he memorised it. He told me that he thought of it every day. And now, of course, he's become part of it.

So when you arrive on the summit, enjoy the Wainwright words and then sit in silence for a while beside the water, and listen for the sigh of contentment that swells on the mountain breeze.

Descents

If you don't want to go back the same way that you came up, the best route down is via Warnscale. (See Haystacks page 6 for details, and page 4 for a map.)

Practical bits

Getting there
Gatesgarth is reached via the B5289, a couple of miles from Buttermere, and accessed via the Honister Pass if you are driving from the east.

Parking
There is parking space opposite Gatesgarth Farm, and more a short way up the Honister Pass. If you are able to extend the walk by a few miles, you could leave your car in one of several car parks in Buttermere, and follow the lovely footpath around the lake to Gatesgarth.

Public transport
This is limited to the 77 Honister Rambler bus, which follows a circular route from Keswick via Whinlatter, Buttermere and Seatoller. It runs four times each day between mid March and late October, and on weekends in November.

General
In the summer, there is a good chance you will find a trailer at Gatesgarth selling ice cream, snacks and drinks. If you don't find it there, Buttermere has a couple of hotels serving food, while Syke House Farm, near the church, has a very good tea room with home-made food including its own ice cream. If you are planning a picnic, it's best to stock up in Keswick or Cockermouth before you reach Gatesgarth.

Haystacks

properly
Hay Stacks
(two words)
as on
Ordnance maps

from Gamlin End, High Crag

Gatesgarth ●
HIGH
▲ CRAG

HAYSTACKS
▲

Black ●Sail Y.H.
MILES
0   1   2

NATURAL FEATURES

Haystacks stands unabashed and unashamed in the midst of a circle of much loftier fells, like a shaggy terrier in the company of foxhounds, some of them known internationally, but not one of this distinguished group of mountains around Ennerdale and Buttermere can show a greater variety and a more fascinating arrangement of interesting features. Here are sharp peaks in profusion, tarns with islands and tarns without islands, crags, screes, rocks for climbing and rocks not for climbing, heather tracts, marshes, serpentine trails, tarns with streams and tarns with no streams.   All these, with a background of magnificent landscapes, await every visitor to Haystacks but they will be appreciated most by those who go there to linger and explore.   It is a place of surprises around corners, and there are many corners.   For a man trying to get a persistent worry out of his mind, the top of Haystacks is a wonderful cure.

The fell rises between the deep hollow of Warnscale Bottom near Gatesgarth, and Ennerdale: between a valley familiar to summer motorists and a valley reached only on foot. It is bounded on the west by Scarth Gap, a pass linking the two. The Buttermere aspect is the better known, although this side is often dark in shadow and seen only as a silhouette against the sky: here, above Warnscale, is a great wall of crags. The Ennerdale flank, open to the sun, is friendlier but steep and rough nevertheless.

Eastwards, beyond the tangle of tors and outcrops forming the boundary of Haystacks on this side, a broad grass slope rises easily and unattractively to Brandreth on the edge of the Borrowdale watershed; beyond is Derwent country.

The spelling of Haystacks as one word is a personal preference of the author (and others), and probably arises from a belief that the name originated from the resemblance of the scattered tors on the summit to stacks of hay in a field. If this were so, the one word *Haystacks* would be correct (as it is in *Haycock*).

But learned authorities state that the name derives from the Icelandic 'stack', meaning 'a columnar rock', and that the true interpretation is *High Rocks*. This is logical and appropriate. *High Rocks* is a name of two words and would be wrongly written as *Highrocks*.

The summit tarn

Big Stack,
looking east from a point near the path to the summit from Scarth Gap.

In the picture below Big Stack appears on the extreme right.

The north crags, looking west from the slopes of Green Crag.

The path is seen skirting the cliff on the left.

MAP

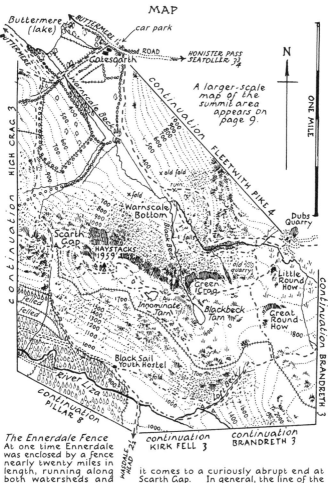

A larger-scale map of the summit area appears on page 9.

The Ennerdale Fence
At one time Ennerdale was enclosed by a fence nearly twenty miles in length, running along both watersheds and around the head of the valley. The fence was mainly of post and wire, and in most places only the posts survive. On Haystacks the fence has been restored, but it comes to a curiously abrupt end at Scarth Gap. In general, the line of the fence followed parish boundaries but on Haystacks there is considerable deviation. Here the series of iron stakes embedded in rock (erected to mark the boundary of the Lonsdale estate) coincides with the parish boundary, but the fence keeps well to the south of this line.

ASCENT FROM GATESGARTH
1550 feet of ascent : 1¼ miles

via SCARTH GAP

HAYSTACKS

Big Stack

Stack Rake

Scarth Gap

HIGH CRAG

From Scarth Gap a well-constructed path leads up to the summit, avoiding all scree, though in places it is necessary to handle rock.

1500

1400

1300

1200

1100

gap

High Wax Knott

Low Wax Knott

It is a test of iron discipline to pass without halting several large *comfortable* boulders athwart the path.

1000

gate

900

700

bracken

800

600

500

400

gap

old sheepfold

Gatesgarth

BUTTERMERE via BURTNESS WOOD

ROAD

car park

Buttermere

Scarth Gap is one of the pleasantest of the foot-passes. Apart from the steep section above the old sheepfold, the gradients are gentle and the views both ahead and behind are full of interest. The path is generally good, and the roughness formerly encountered on the early stages of the climb is buried underneath a new conifer plantation.

Leave Gatesgarth by the bridge, at a signpost to Ennerdale.

Coupled with a return by the Warnscale route to make a full 'round' journey, the ascent of Haystacks via the pass of Scarth Gap is a prelude of much merit and beauty to a mountain walk of unique character, the whole distance being no more than five miles. Save it, however, for a fine clear day.

looking south

ASCENT FROM GATESGARTH
via WARNSCALE
1600 feet of ascent · 2¾ miles

HAYSTACKS

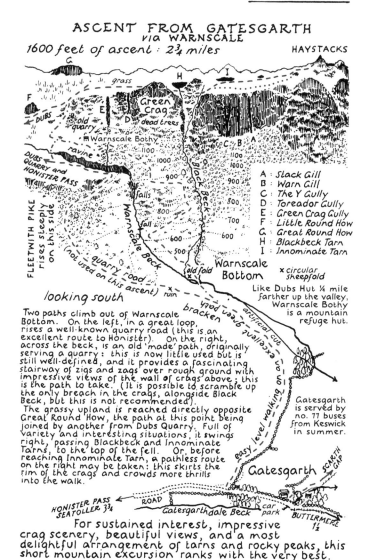

looking south

A : Slack Gill
B : Warn Gill
C : The Y Gully
D : Toreador Gully
E : Green Crag Gully
F : Little Round How
G : Great Round How
H : Blackbeck Tarn
I : Innominate Tarn

x circular sheepfold

Like Dubs Hut ¼ mile farther up the valley, Warnscale Bothy is a mountain refuge hut.

Two paths climb out of Warnscale Bottom. On the left, in a great loop, rises a well-known quarry road (this is an excellent route to Honister). On the right, across the beck, is an old 'made' path, originally serving a quarry: this is now little used but is still well-defined, and it provides a fascinating stairway of zigs and zags over rough ground with impressive views of the wall of crags above; this is the path to take. (It is possible to scramble up the only breach in the crags, alongside Black Beck, but this is not recommended).
The grassy upland is reached directly opposite Great Round How, the path at this point being joined by another from Dubs Quarry. Full of variety and interesting situations, it swings right, passing Blackbeck and Innominate Tarns, to the top of the fell. Or, before reaching Innominate Tarn, a pathless route on the right may be taken: this skirts the rim of the crags and crowds more thrills into the walk.

Gatesgarth is served by no. 77 buses from Keswick in summer.

For sustained interest, impressive crag scenery, beautiful views, and a most delightful arrangement of tarns and rocky peaks, this short mountain excursion ranks with the very best.

ASCENT FROM HONISTER PASS
1050 feet of ascent : 2¼ miles

A note of explanation is required.   This ascent-route does not conform to the usual pattern, being more in the nature of an upland cross-country walk than a mountain climb : there are two pronounced descents before foot is set on Haystacks. The wide variety of scene and the fascinating intricacies of the path are justification for the inclusion of the route in this book.

If returning to Honister, note the path to Brandreth just below Innominate Tarn. It is marked by a cairn, but it is very difficult to follow. By using this until it joins the Great Gable path and then swinging left around Dubs Bottom, the Drum House can be regained without extra effort or time.

After traversing the back of Green Crag the path drops to the outlet of Blackbeck Tarn, rising stonily therefrom with a profound abyss on the right. This section is the highlight of the walk.

HAYSTACKS

tarn — 1800

Innominate Tarn

BRANDRETH

Blackbeck Tarn

Green Crag

Great Round How — 1600

Little Round How

grass

WARNSCALE BOTTOM

Dubs Bottom

stepping stones

1500

1400

WARNSCALE BOTTOM

1500

1600

Dubs Quarry (disused)

BRANDRETH GREAT GABLE

looking west

1700

foundations of Drum House

1700

old tramway

1600

1500

1400

rock cutting

1300

1200

quarry road

Honister Slate Mine

BUTTERMERE

Honister Pass 1190'

From the hut at Dubs Quarry leave the road and go down to the stream, crossing it (by stepping stones) where its silent meanderings through the Dubs marshes assume a noisy urgency.

From the top of Honister Pass Haystacks is nowhere in sight, and even when it comes into view, after crossing the shoulder of Fleetwith Pike at the Drum House, it is insignificant against the towering background of Pillar, being little higher in altitude and seemingly remote across the wide depression of Dubs Bottom. But, although the route here described is not a natural approach, the elevation of Honister Pass, its car-parking facilities, and the unerring pointer of the tramway make access to Haystacks particularly convenient from this point.

ASCENT FROM ENNERDALE
(BLACK SAIL YOUTH HOSTEL)

970 feet of ascent
1¼ miles

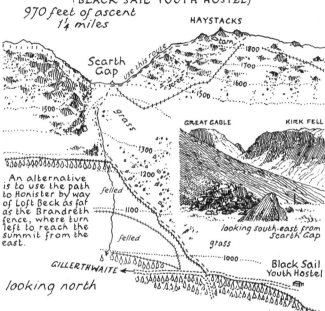

HAYSTACKS

Scarth Gap

use this route

tarn

1800
1700
1600
1500

scree

1500

1500

grass

1300

1200

felled

1100

felled

grass

GREAT GABLE   KIRK FELL

looking south-east from Scarth Gap

An alternative is to use the path to Honister by way of Loft Beck as far as the Brandreth fence, where turn left to reach the summit from the east.

1000

Black Sail Youth Hostel

GILLERTHWAITE ←

looking north

This route is likely to be of interest only to those staying at the magnificently situated Black Sail Youth Hostel. This hostel is open to everyone, but those intending to use it are advised to book well in advance.

formerly a shepherd's hut,.....

Black Sail Youth Hostel

THE SUMMIT

ONE MILE

N

GATESGARTH
BUTTERMERE

Scarth
Gap

ENNERDALE

viewpoint

GATESGARTH

DUBS for
HONISTER

Green Crag

old
quarry

Little
Round
How

1600

1500

1600

1800

Innominate
Tarn

PLAN OF THE TOP

Blackbeck
Tarn

1600

Great
Round
How

1700

1800

perched
boulder

1700

The highest part of the
fell is a small rocky ridge,
fifty yards in length, with
a cairn at each end and a
tarn alongside to the west. The
two cairns are at approximately
the same elevation, but the north
one, lying on the line of the path
across the top of the fell, is usually
regarded as the true summit. Its height
is currently reckoned to be 1959 feet.

stiles

stile

1700   1700

ENNERDALE

continued

THE SUMMIT

continued

Haystacks fails to qualify for inclusion in the author's "best half-dozen" only because of inferior height, a deficiency in vertical measurement. Another thousand feet would have made all the difference.

But for beauty, variety and interesting detail, for sheer fascination and unique individuality, the summit-area of Haystacks is supreme. This is in fact the best fell-top of all — a place of great charm and fairyland attractiveness. Seen from a distance, these qualities are not suspected: indeed, on the contrary, the appearance of Haystacks is almost repellent when viewed from the higher surrounding peaks: black are its bones and black is its flesh. With its thick covering of heather it is dark and sombre even when the sun sparkles the waters of its many tarns, gloomy and mysterious even under a blue sky. There are fierce crags and rough screes and outcrops that will be grittier still when the author's ashes are scattered here.*

Yet the combination of features, of tarn and tor, of cliff and cove, the labyrinth of corners and recesses, the maze of old sheepwalks and paths, form a design, or a lack of design, of singular appeal and absorbing interest. One can forget even a raging toothache on Haystacks.

✳ After his death in 1991, Wainwright's ashes were duly scattered on Haystacks.

perched boulder on a rock platform

Note the profile in shadow. Some women have faces like that.

On a first visit, learn thoroughly the details of the mile-long main path across the top, a magnificent traverse, because this serves as the best introduction to the geography of the fell.

Having memorised this, several interesting deviations may be made: the parallel alternative above the rim of the north face, the scramble onto Big Stack, the 'cross-country' route around the basin of Blackbeck Tarn, the walk alongside the fence, and so on.

typical summit tors

DESCENTS: A well-made path starts just west of the summit and leads down to Scarth Gap. An alternative path farther south is marred by loose stones and should be avoided. It is advisable to regard the whole of the north edge as highly dangerous. The only advice that can be given to a novice lost on Haystacks *in mist* is that he should kneel down and pray for safe deliverance.

THE VIEW

This is not a case of distance lending enchantment to the view, because apart from a glimpse of Skiddaw above the Robinson-Hindscarth depression and a slice of the Helvellyn range over Honister, the scene is predominantly one of high mountains within a five-mile radius. And really good they look — the enchantment is close at hand. Set in a tight surround, they are seen in revealing detail: a rewarding study deserving leisurely appreciation.

Principal Fells

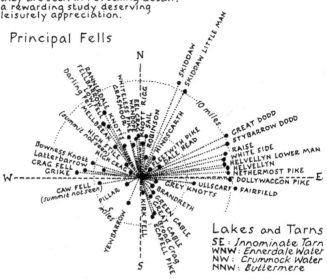

Lakes and Tarns

SE: *Innominate Tarn*
WNW: *Ennerdale Water*
NW: *Crummock Water*
NNW: *Buttermere*

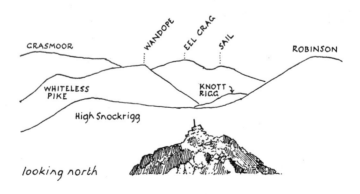

looking north

RIDGE ROUTES

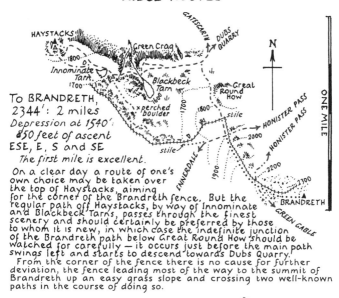

To BRANDRETH, 2344′: 2 miles
Depression at 1540′:
850 feet of ascent
ESE, E, S and SE

The first mile is excellent.

On a clear day a route of one's own choice may be taken over the top of Haystacks, aiming for the corner of the Brandreth fence. But the regular path off Haystacks, by way of Innominate and Blackbeck Tarns, passes through the finest scenery and should certainly be preferred by those to whom it is new, in which case the indefinite junction of the Brandreth path below Great Round How should be watched for carefully — it occurs just before the main path swings left and starts to descend towards Dubs Quarry.

From the corner of the fence there is no cause for further deviation, the fence leading most of the way to the summit of Brandreth up an easy grass slope and crossing two well-known paths in the course of doing so.

To HIGH CRAG, 2443′
1¼ miles : W, then NW
Depression at 1425′ (Scarth Gap)
1100 feet of ascent
A fine walk in spite of scree

Follow faithfully the well-made path to the west from the summit, a delightful game of ins and outs and ups and downs. An alternative path south of the summit encounters an area of loose stones and should be avoided. From Scarth Gap a beautiful path climbs through the heather to

High Crag, from Scarth Gap

Seat; then a good ridge follows to the final tower of High Crag: this deteriorates badly into slippery scree on the later stages of the ascent.

HALF A MILE

4 Helm Crag
from Grasmere

I'm told there are certain snooty souls who write off Helm Crag as a mere trippers' hill. A hill for amateurs who've climbed off the tourist buses in Grasmere. Certainly not a place for us 'professional' fell walkers to waste our time.

Well, let me tell you that they're entirely wrong.

Helm Crag is welcoming as a good host is welcoming. It accepts visitors for what they are. It gives the brash a platform on which to perform, but there are nooks and crannies where shyer visitors can wedge themselves to admire the summit panoramas. It gives instant gratification in its views over Grasmere and Loughrigg, but also more subtle compositions. Steel Fell, turning gold to deep, bracken orange, with Helm Crag's summit rocks stark grey black in the foreground. The Langdale Pikes above Easedale Tarn, and cloud shadows racing across the great bowl of hills that's Far Easdale.

Trippers indeed.

Helm Crag is also extremely proud that it's the only one of Wainwright's 214 Lakeland summits where he failed to get to the top. He bottled out when it came to climbing to the very pinnacle of Helm Crag's tallest pillar of shattered rock. AW eschewed any ascent that needed rope or ironwork, sticky fingers or potentially dangerous athleticism. But the mountain still welcomes climbers as well as humble scramblers like us.

Wainwright went to Helm Crag many times, it being one of his lower-level bolt holes when he was weathered off the higher fells. But one of the days he made it (almost) to the top, he was in pensive mood. He was having intimations of human stupidity. (Helm Crag welcomes both the philosopher and the visitor with not a thought in his head.) As AW sat there that wintry day, he mused about the future of his books and the future of the fells. He decided that the views would probably remain unaltered for ever, 'assuming that falling satellites and other fancy gadgets of man's invention don't blow God's far worthier creations to bits'. But the books, he decided that day, would probably just fade away:

> ... and because I should just hate to see my name on anything that could not be relied on, the probability is that the books will progressively be withdrawn from publication after a currency of a few years.

That was a day in 1958. He'd only finished three of the seven guides. Half a century later, they're still with us and with only minor revisions. And AW's boundless enthusiasm still shines from their pages.

> ... I walked on golden carpets between golden tap-estries, marvelling anew at the supreme crafts-manship that had created so great a loveliness, and at my own good fortune to be in its midst, enjoying a heaven I had done nothing to deserve.

Whether you're feeling unworthy or in full poetic flow, you'll find a welcome on Helm Crag.

Descents
As Wainwright explains on page 4, this is one of the few fells where ascent and descent by the same route

are recommended. There are alternatives, shown on the map on page 3, but there is nothing to be said in their favour.

Practical bits

Parking
The roads in and around Grasmere are congested during the summer season, but you should always be able to find space in one of the several car parks. If the central one is full, the Stock Lane car park at the southern end of the village is a short stroll from the start of this walk.

Public transport
The 555 Lakeslink bus linking Carlisle and Lancaster calls at Grasmere every hour on its way through the Lakes. From mid March to late August, the 599 bus service, usually open-topped, runs to Grasmere from Windermere, Bowness and Ambleside.

General
Refreshment in Grasmere is a choice between a few hotel or pub bars and several cafés. There is a bakery on Red Lion Square plus a small supermarket and plenty of other shops stocking food and drink for picnics – and don't forget to pick up some of Grasmere's famous gingerbread for the walk, from Sarah Nelson's shop near the church.

Helm Crag

1329'

affectionately known as 'The Lion and The Lamb'

HELM ▲
CRAG

Grasmere ●

MILES
0 1 2

This is the smallest (and most accurate!) map in the book

from Grasmere

NATURAL FEATURES

Helm Crag may well be the best-known of all Lakeland fells, and possibly even the best-known hill in the country. Generations of waggonette and motor-coach tourists have been tutored to recognise its appearance in the Grasmere landscape: it is the one feature of their Lakeland tour they hail at sight, and in unison, but the cry on their lips is not "Helm Crag!" but "The Lion and the Lamb!" — in a variety of dialects. The resemblance of the summit rocks to a lion is so striking that recognition, from several viewpoints, is instant; yet, oddly, the outline most like Leo is not the official 'Lion' at all: in fact there are two lions, each with a lamb, and each guards one end of the summit ridge as though set there by architectural design. The summit is altogether a rather weird and fantastic place, well worth not merely a visit but a detailed and leisurely exploration. Indeed the whole fell, although of small extent, is unusually interesting; its very appearance is challenging; its sides are steep, rough and craggy; its top bristles; it *looks* irascible, like a shaggy terrier in a company of sleek foxhounds, for all around are loftier and smoother fells, circling the pleasant vale of Grasmere out of which Helm Crag rises so abruptly.

The fell is not isolated, nor independent of others, for it is the termination of a long ridge enclosing Far Easedale in a graceful curve on north and east and rising, finally, to the rocky peak of Calf Crag. It drains quickly, is dry underfoot, and has no streams worthy of mention.

The virtues of Helm Crag have not been lauded enough. It gives an exhilarating little climb, a brief essay in real mountaineering, and, in a region where all is beautiful, it makes a notable contribution to the natural charms and attractions of Grasmere.

outline of STEEL FELL

DUNMAIL RAISE

THE GREENBURN VALLEY

summit scene

MAP

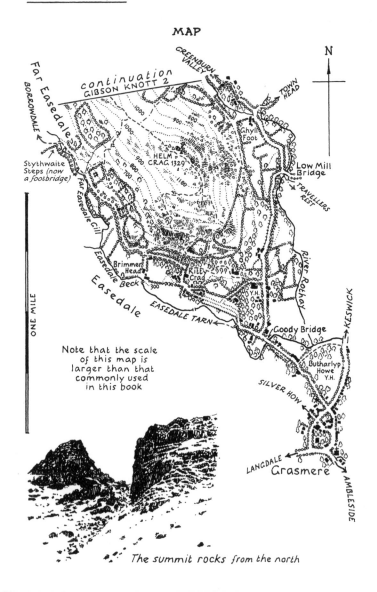

N

GREENBURN VALLEY

continuation
GIBSON KNOTT 2

Far Easedale

BORROWDALE

TOWN HEAD

Ghyll Foot

1000
900
800

HELM CRAG 1329

Low Mill Bridge

Stythwaite Steps (now a footbridge)

900
800
700

1100

TRAVELLERS REST

Far Easedale Gill

River Rothay

Easedale Beck

Brimmer Head

Riley Crag

300

Y.H.

KESWICK

Easedale

EASEDALE TARN

Goody Bridge

Butharlyp Howe Y.H.

SILVER HOW

ONE MILE

Note that the scale
of this map is
larger than that
commonly used
in this book

LANGDALE
Grasmere

AMBLESIDE

The summit rocks from the north

ASCENT FROM GRASMERE
1100 feet of ascent : 1½ miles

HELM CRAG

bracken

1200·

new path

1000

900

White Crag

900

Raven Crag

bracken

800

scree

700

800

Jackdaw Crag

old path

700

600

600

600

Lancrigg Crag

600

500

Kitty Crag

400

300

FAR EASEDALE & BORROWDALE (footpath)

Easedale

EASEDALE TARN

LOW MILL BRIDGE and GHYLL FOOT

Goody Bridge

Easedale Beck

Butharlyp Howe Y.H.

studio

LANGDALE

KESWICK

Red Lion Hotel

car park

Grasmere

Church

looking north-west

This is one of the few hills where ascent and descent by the same route is recommended, the new path depicted here being much the best way both up and down. An alternative route (shown on the map but not on this diagram) has nothing in its favour.

If, however, Helm Crag is to be a part only of the day's programme (e.g. the circuit of Far Easedale or the Greenburn valley) it is better reserved for descent, for then the Vale of Grasmere will be directly in view ahead; and this fair scene is at its best when the shadows of evening are lengthening, with the Langdales silhouetted in rugged outline against the sunset. Tarry long over this exquisite picture of serenity and peace, and memorise it for the long winter of exile!

This is a splendid little climb; if it has a fault it is that it is too short. But for the evening of the day of arrival in Grasmere on a walking holiday it is just the thing: an epitome of Lakeland concentrated in the space of two hours — and an excellent foretaste of happy days to come.

THE SUMMIT

Rocks at the north-west
end of the summit ridge,
known by various names:
(a) The Lion Couchant,
or, more popularly, The
Lion and The Lamb.
(as seen from the road
below Dunmail Raise)
(b) The Howitzer
(as seen from
Dunmail Raise)

The highest
point of the
rocks is the
true summit
of the fell

In scenic values, the summits of many high mountains are a disappointment after the long toil of ascent, yet here, on the top of little Helm Crag, a midget of a mountain, is a remarkable array of rocks, upstanding and fallen, of singular interest and fascinating appearance, that yield a quality of reward out of all proportion to the short and simple climb. The uppermost inches of Scafell and Helvellyn and Skiddaw can show nothing like Helm Crag's crown of shattered and petrified stone : indeed, its highest point, a pinnacle of rock airily thrust out above a dark abyss, is not to be attained by walking and is brought underfoot only by precarious manœuvres of the body. This is one of the very few summits in Lakeland reached only by climbing rocks, and it is certainly (but not for that reason alone) one of the very best.

continued

THE SUMMIT

continued

The summit ridge is 250 yards in length and is adorned at each end by fangs of rock overtopping the fairly level path. Between these towers there have been others in ages past but all that remains of them now is a chaos of collapsed boulders, choking a strange depression that extends the full length of the summit on the north-east side. The depression is bounded by a secondary ridge, and this in turn descends craggily to an even more strange depression, in appearance resembling a huge ditch cleft straight as a furrow across the breast of the fell for 300 yards; or, more romantically, a deep moat defending the turreted wall of the castle above. This surprising feature, which will not be seen unless searched for, will doubtless be readily explained by geologists (or antiquaries?); to the unlearned beholder it seems likely to be the result of some ancient natural convulsion that caused the side of the fell to slip downwards a few yards before coming to rest. This ditch is also bounded on its far side by a parallel ridge or parapet (narrow, and an interesting walk) beyond which the fellside plunges down almost precipitously to the valley, falling in juniper-clad crags.

Care is necessary when exploring the boulder-strewn depressions on the summit, especially if the rocks are greasy. There are many good natural shelters here, and some dangerous clefts and fissures and holes, so well protected from the weather that summer flowers are to be found in bloom in their recesses as late as mid-winter.

The south-west side of the summit ridge consists mainly of bracken slopes and are of little interest in their upper reaches.

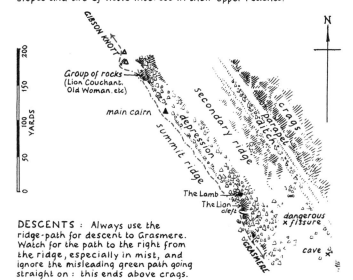

DESCENTS : Always use the ridge-path for descent to Grasmere. Watch for the path to the right from the ridge, especially in mist, and ignore the misleading green path going straight on : this ends above crags.

THE SUMMIT

Rocks at the north-west end of the summit-ridge
known as The Old Woman
Playing the Organ *from
their appearance when
seen from Tongue Gill
and the vicinity of
Easedale Tarn*

Rocks at the south-east
end of the summit-ridge.
These form the OFFICIAL
Lion *and* The Lamb
*(as seen from the Swan
Hotel, Grasmere). The
lion's head is the O.S.
'station' (altitude 1306')
but is not quite the
highest point of the fell*

THE VIEW

This is the view from the cairn on the summit ridge — whether it coincides with the view from the highest point the author will never know for his several attempts to mount to the rocky pate of the Lion Couchant have all been defeated by a lack of resolution; but probably it is the same. In any case, most visitors will be content to study the prospect from the comparative security of the cairn on the ridge.

continued

continued
The Vale of Grasmere is best displayed from the head of the other (official) Lion, which even the author found a simple ascent, (although deeply conscious of precipices all around).

Principal Fells

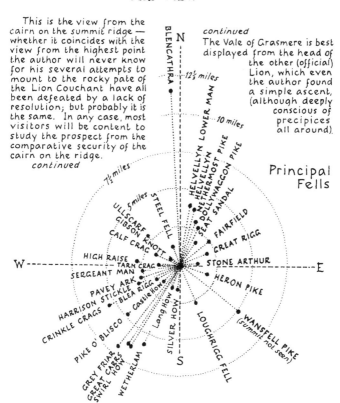

The prominent height south-south-east (to the right of Loughrigg Fell) is Gummer's How, 13 miles distant at the foot of Windermere.

Lakes and Tarns

SE : *Windermere (upper reach)*
SSE : *Grasmere*
SSE : *Esthwaite Water*
WSW : *Easedale Tarn*

This corner was reserved for an announcement that the author had succeeded in surmounting the highest point, but no such announcement was made.

Tarn Crag
across Far Easedale
from the slopes of Helm Crag

The north-east face
from Low Mill Bridge

RIDGE ROUTE

To GIBSON KNOTT, 1379'
1 mile : NW, then W
Depression at 1050'
400 feet of ascent
An interesting ridge climb

Two big cairns indicate the way off
Helm Crag. A narrow path crosses the
depression and continues up the opposite
slope; it does not keep to the ridge, but
crosses it from left to right and back again,
winding charmingly between rock outcrops.
The cairned summit rises across a shallow hollow.

ONE MILE

Helm Crag, from the path to Gibson Knott

5 Latrigg
from Keswick

Of the 214 Wainwright summits in Lakeland, Latrigg is the smallest. Just 1203 feet to be precise. But it's a summit that you shouldn't attempt in poor visibility. That's not because of any danger to life and limb, because Latrigg is the sort of gentle summit you could almost do in your sleep – just so long as you can also read a map and compass in your sleep, of course. No, the reason for avoiding Latrigg in poor visibility is that you would have to kick yourself so hard when you got to the top because of missing one of Lakeland's greatest views. In fact, it's a place where landscape and imagination coincide.

Just imagine if you'd been able to sit on Latrigg and watch the activity away to your left when the Castlerigg stone circle was in regular use. There's a wonderful view of it from up here and you'd have been able to put answers to all those questions and mysteries that persist about it. Was it built for reasons of religion or astronomy, mathematics or trade? Was there a priestly, druidical sect that were guardians of the circle?

Imagine, too, being able to look down to the rooftops of Keswick and watch a steam locomotive on the CKP railway arrive with a full train of excited visitors at the iron-and-glass canopied station.

A hundred years earlier you would have been able to look out over Derwent Water, just beyond the town, and watch the Duke of Portland's yacht sail up the lake. From time to time there would have been the re-verberating echo of the yacht's cannon, fired to delight the fashionable passengers who'd paid a fortune for the privilege.

It was a rather more peaceful place in the seventh century. Imagine the year 686. From up here on the shoulder of Latrigg you could have seen a small boat approaching an island on Derwent Water. It was bringing St Cuthbert of Lindisfarne to visit his friend St Herbert, who lived a life of solitude in a hermitage on the island. During that visit the two men agreed to leave this life together. Cuthbert returned to Holy Island a few days later and they had no further contact, but they both died on 20 March 687.

At the beginning of the twentieth century, if you'd had a particularly good set of binoculars you might just have caught a glimpse of a strange craft with a square-cut sail, steered along the lake by a rather battered and rangy old gentleman wearing a boy-scout hat. That would have been Millican Dalton, self-styled Professor of Adventure who offered visitors to the valley camping holidays and 'hair's breadth escapes'. He'd been a London insurance clerk who dropped out and lived in a set of caves on Castle Crag in the Jaws of Borrowdale. His motto can still be seen carved on a rock at the cave entrance. It says 'Don't waste words. Jump to conclusions.' I'd like to have met him.

Of course, if all this imagination business is getting to be a bit tiring you can always just prop yourself up on one elbow on the comfortable turf of Latrigg and do what Alfred Wainwright used to do. If the light and weather were right, the plans for the day would often be put on hold and he would take time to relish the view and recharge the batteries. Borrowdale and the Newlands Valley sinking into the glories of a Lakeland evening. The last of the sun occasionally bursting through pink-tinged cloud. Tomorrow we'll tackle something a bit bigger, but for the moment, who could wish for anything better than Latrigg?

Descents
If you don't want to go down the same way that you came up, there are various alternatives detailed on Latrigg page 5, but none is especially recommended.

Practical bits

Getting there
Keswick is well connected by road – the A66 takes you to and from the M6, and the A591 links it with the southern Lakes – but traffic in the town can be very slow and parking difficult.

Parking
Central car parks are small and fill up quickly on sunny days; arrive promptly in the morning, if you can, and try Victoria Street or Heads Road first. Or save on parking costs and take the bus instead.

Public transport
The 555 Lakeslink bus calls at Keswick every hour or so on its way between the north and south of Cumbria, while the 73 (Carlisle, Caldbeck, Hesket Newmarket), the 77 (Buttermere, Borrowdale), the 79 (Borrowdale) and the 208 (Patterdale, Glenridding, Troutbeck) also stop in the town. Services vary from

season to season, so it's worth contacting Cumbria's Traveline for times and advice in advance (telephone 0871 200 22 33 or online at www.traveline.info).

General
Wherever you are in Keswick, you won't have to go far to find food and drink. There are dozens of cafés, pubs and restaurants, and a Booths supermarket and other shops for picnic essentials.

Latrigg

1203'

This is the Latrigg near Keswick
— there is another,
less well·known,
near Over Water.

from the Blencathra Centre
*(showing the east ridge going
down to Brundholme Woods)*

▲ SKIDDAW

▲ LITTLE MAN

▲ LONSCALE FELL

● Millbeck

Threlkeld ●

▲ LATRIGG

● Keswick

MILES

0 1 2 3 4

from the Orthwaite road

NATURAL FEATURES

Latrigg is to Keswick what Loughrigg is to Ambleside and Helm Crag to Grasmere : a small hill, an excellent viewpoint, a great favourite of local folk and visitors. Latrigg is pastoral and parkland in character, not rough fell, and the summit is the easiest of promenades, so that this is not a climb calling for old clothes and heavy boots : 'Sunday best' is quite appropriate dress. The woods, once a haven for courting couples and other wildlife, are privately owned, being part of the Mirehouse Estate, and in recent years they have been increasingly managed for the benefit of walkers. There are three information panels, and a circular walk has been created. It heads east from Spoony Green for two miles and returns at a lower level. A leaflet is available at the Tourist Information Centre in Keswick.

Latrigg has been well described as 'the cub of Skiddaw'. It crouches at the foot of the broad southern slopes of the parent, too small to be significant in the geography of the mass, although a long east ridge is reponsible for the formation of the short side-valley of Lonscale. The River Greta flows along the southern base, occupying a wooded gorge of outstanding scenic beauty, appreciated best from the disused railway from Keswick to Threlkeld.

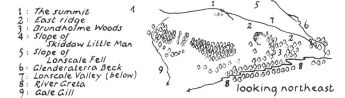

1 : The summit
2 : East ridge
3 : Brundholme Woods
4 : Slope of
    Skiddaw Little Man
5 : Slope of
    Lonscale Fell
6 : Glenderaterra Beck
7 : Lonscale Valley (below)
8 : River Greta
9 : Gale Gill

looking northeast

Latrigg's top is a smooth grassy pasture innocent of rock except for a few yards of outcrop at the summit where the native stone breaks through the turf. This is seen to be slate. The wall across the top to the east is built of slate.

Not long ago, in fact since the turn of the 20th century, Latrigg's top was described as having a scattering of boulders of volcanic rock deposited there by a retreating glacier. These boulders were identified as having their origin in the crags of Clough Head and it is therefore simple to reconstruct (but difficult to imagine) the scene here at the end of the Ice Age : the glacier tore from its moorings in the narrows of St. John's Vale, and, taking the route of the present St. John's Beck and River Greta and being joined by tributaries of ice from the Glenderamackin, the Glenderaterra and the Naddle Valleys, slowly withdrew from the hills, scouring the side of Lonscale Fell and Skiddaw and depositing the rubble collected on its journey as it disintegrated. The presence of Clough Head rocks on the top of Latrigg indicates that the surface of the glacier must have been higher than the present elevation of the fell.

These boulders have now gone, possibly removed with the trees to make a smooth sheepwalk. Just a few 'erratics' can still be found by diligent search, but the evidence of the movement of the glacier is more abundant lower down the fellside and about the bed of the Greta, where, to a trained eye, there are several manifestations of glacial action, much of it unearthed during the construction of the railway.

MAP

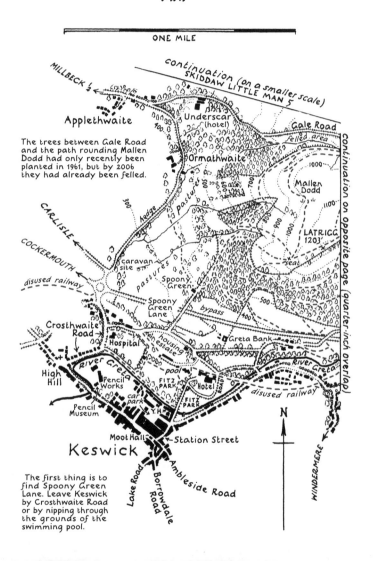

ONE MILE

continuation (on a smaller scale)
SKIDDAW LITTLE MAN 5

MILLBECK ½

Applethwaite

Underscar (hotel)

Gale Road

felled area

The trees between Gale Road and the path rounding Mallen Dodd had only recently been planted in 1961, but by 2006 they had already been felled.

Ormathwaite

Mallen Dodd

continuation on opposite page (quarter-inch overlap)

CARLISLE

COCKERMOUTH

disused railway

hedge

pasture

300

LATRIGG 1203'

seat

caravan site

pastures

Spoony Green

Spoony Green Lane

bypass

Crosthwaite Road →

Hospital

housing estate

Greta Bank

500

400

pool

River Greta

High Hill

Pencil Works

car park

Pencil Museum

FITZ PARK

FITZ PARK

Hotel

River Greta

disused railway

Y.H.I.

N

Moot Hall ← Station Street

Keswick

Lake Road

Borrowdale Road

Ambleside Road

WINDERMERE

The first thing is to find Spoony Green Lane. Leave Keswick by Crosthwaite Road or by nipping through the grounds of the swimming pool.

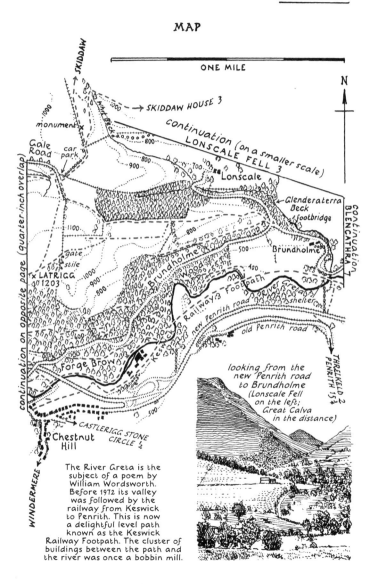

MAP

ONE MILE

N

SKIDDAW

→ SKIDDAW HOUSE 3

continuation (on a smaller scale)
LONSCALE FELL 3

monument ×

Gale
Road

car
park

1000

800

900

800

Lonscale

Glenderaterra
Beck
footbridge

continuation on opposite page (quarter-inch overlap)

continuation BLENCATHRA 7

Gale
stile

1100

800

Brundholme
Wood

500

Brundholme

× LATRIGG
1203

1000

800

Railway Footpath

400

River Greta

shelter

new Penrith road

old Penrith road

THRELKELD 2
PENRITH 15¼

Keswick

Forge Brow

500

CASTLERIGG STONE
CIRCLE ½

Chestnut
Hill

WINDERMERE

looking from the
new Penrith road
to Brundholme
(Lonscale Fell
on the left;
Great Calva
in the distance)

The River Greta is the
subject of a poem by
William Wordsworth.
Before 1972 its valley
was followed by the
railway from Keswick
to Penrith. This is now
a delightful level path
known as the Keswick
Railway Footpath. The cluster of
buildings between the path and
the river was once a bobbin mill.

ASCENT FROM KESWICK
950 feet of ascent: 2½ miles

The original path, rounding Mallen Dodd, is the easiest route to the top, but there are a number of short-cuts. The start of Route A is easily missed. It leaves the main path by a gate post at the end of a short stretch of fence. For Route B turn sharp right onto a forest road and then turn left after passing through a gate. This route is best avoided because of a difficult stretch just below the fence. Route C leaves the main path shortly after it crosses a stream. All these paths are provided with stiles where they cross the forest fence. At the time of writing this is a good place to see red squirrels, but in a few years they will probably all be gone.

Happily, the superb view from the summit is available also to non-climbers, and the old and infirm, with the assistance of a car, can enjoy it by a simple stroll from the road end.

Road end
Cars may be taken to this point (via Underscar) and parked here

SKIDDAW

Gale Road UNDERSCAR

gate post   Mallen Dodd

LATRIGG

grass

1100

seat

ridge

1000

C   B

A

900

800

700

500

looking east

Ewe How (viewpoint)

gate post

bypass

Just above Spoony Green is an interesting notice board with paintings of wildlife and information about Latrigg Woods.

Spoony Green

Spoony Green Lane

CARLISLE

housing estate

There is a bewildering choice of paths, that by Mallen Dodd being best. The descent by the east ridge and return to Keswick by Brundholme Woods completes a very beautiful short walk.

Pheasant Inn

Crosthwaite Road

Hospital

River Greta

Keswick

ASCENT FROM THRELKELD
900 feet of ascent : 3 miles

This simple climb by the east ridge can be made with equal facility from Keswick. Take the road behind the swimming pool signposted "Windebrowe & Brundholme" — this degenerates into a lane but improves in scenery as it enters and passes through the woods: a delightful walk with interesting glimpses of the River Greta below.

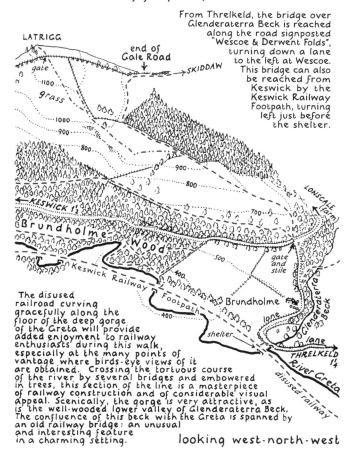

From Threlkeld, the bridge over Glenderaterra Beck is reached along the road signposted "Wescoe & Derwent Folds", turning down a lane to the left at Wescoe. This bridge can also be reached from Keswick by the Keswick Railway Footpath, turning left just before the shelter.

The disused railroad curving gracefully along the floor of the deep gorge of the Greta will provide added enjoyment to railway enthusiasts during this walk, especially at the many points of vantage where birds-eye views of it are obtained. Crossing the tortuous course of the river by several bridges and embowered in trees, this section of the line is a masterpiece of railway construction and of considerable visual appeal. Scenically, the gorge is very attractive, as is the well-wooded lower valley of Glenderaterra Beck. The confluence of this beck with the Greta is spanned by an old railway bridge: an unusual and interesting feature in a charming setting.

looking west-north-west

Underskiddaw, looking to Bassenthwaite Lake

......Two views from Latrigg......

Blease Fell, Blencathra, from the east ridge

THE SUMMIT

The top of Latrigg is a green sward, crossed by an excellent gravel path that runs along the top of a causeway. 150 yards west of the summit the path passes almost over the top of a little rocky knoll where there are good views of Keswick and Derwent Water. 100 yards farther west is a seat in a commanding position bearing the inscription 'a 90th birthday tribute to Ronald Lupton of Keswick 23/7/91'. The area was once covered in trees, but now only a pine and two larches remain; even the stumps have gone.

The top of Latrigg is a grand place, especially for fellwalkers on the retired list: here they can recline for hours, recalling joyful days when they had energy enough to climb to the tops of all the mountains in view. Strange how all the best days of memory are to do with summit-cairns....... Will there be mountains like these in heaven...... or is *this* heaven, before death, and will there never again be hills to climb? Is Latrigg the last of all? But no, it needn't be — there's still Orrest Head, even easier...... Funny, *that's* where we came in ......

CAUSEY PIKE   BARROW   SCAR CRAGS   SAIL   EEL CRAG   OUTERSIDE   GRASMOOR   Coledale House   GRISEDALE PIKE

The Grasmoor group, from Gale Road

THE VIEW

There is complete contrast between the northern and southern halves of the view. The northern, consisting of featureless slopes sweeping up to a high skyline, will hardly get a second glance unless the ling is in bloom, but to the south is a panorama of crowded detail, all of it of great beauty: indeed, this scene is one of the gems of the district. The roofs of Keswick are below, Derwent Water is set out just beyond, in its lovely entirety, and in the distance Borrowdale and the Newlands Valley are seen winding deeply amongst the sombre mountains. The far horizon is a jumbled upheaval of peaks, with many dear old friends standing up proudly: Helvellyn, Bowfell, the Scafells, Great Gable, Pillar, the Buttermere fells, and, much nearer, the striking outline of the Grasmoor group. There is enough of interest in this charming picture to engage the attention for many hours, and Latrigg is a place to visit time and time again, for the scene is never quite the same but always fresh and exciting. The view is so much the best reason for climbing Latrigg that it is almost a pity to make the ascent on a day of poor visibility.

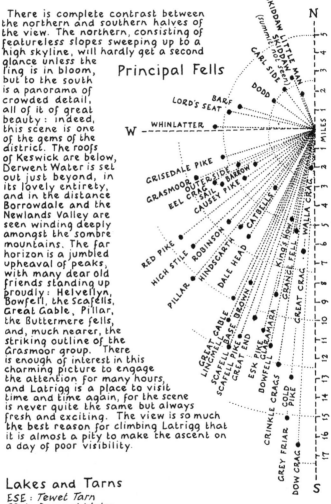

Principal Fells

Lakes and Tarns
ESE : *Tewet Tarn*
SSW : *Derwent Water*
NW : *Bassenthwaite Lake*

THE VIEW

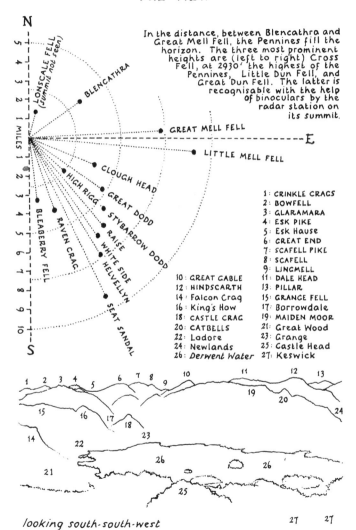

In the distance, between Blencathra and Great Mell Fell, the Pennines fill the horizon. The three most prominent heights are (left to right) Cross Fell, at 2930' the highest of the Pennines, Little Dun Fell, and Great Dun Fell. The latter is recognisable with the help of binoculars by the radar station on its summit.

N

5 4 3 2 1 MILES 1 2 3 4 5 6 7 8 9 10

S

LONSCALE FELL (summit not seen)

BLENCATHRA

GREAT MELL FELL

LITTLE MELL FELL

E

CLOUGH HEAD

HIGH RIGG

GREAT DODD

STYBARROW DODD

RAISE

WHITE SIDE

HELVELLYN

SEAT SANDAL

RAVEN CRAG

BLEABERRY FELL

1: CRINKLE CRAGS
2: BOWFELL
3: GLARAMARA
4: ESK PIKE
5: Esk Hause
6: GREAT END
7: SCAFELL PIKE
8: SCAFELL
9: LINGMELL
10: GREAT GABLE
11: DALE HEAD
12: HINDSCARTH
13: PILLAR
14: Falcon Crag
15: GRANGE FELL
16: King's How
17: Borrowdale
18: CASTLE CRAG
19: MAIDEN MOOR
20: CATBELLS
21: Great Wood
22: Ladore
23: Grange
24: Newlands
25: Castle Head
26: *Derwent Water*
27: Keswick

looking south-south-west

6 Nab Scar
from Grasmere

Hardened fell walkers will know Nab Scar as the start or finish of the Fairfield Horseshoe, nobody ever having decided which was the 'proper' way to do that circuit (if indeed there needs to be a proper way). But for those doing the whole route, Nab Scar is just a warmer-upper before Heron Pike, Great Rigg, Fairfield itself, Hart Crag, Dove Crag and High and Low Pikes. Ten miles or so of bracing high-level walking. But even if you don't feel up to the big challenge, Nab Scar will get the pulse going and offer up some lovely vistas and poetic associations.

We're in the heart of Wordsworth territory here. On the way out to Nab Scar we pass Rydal Mount, where William and his family lived from 1813 to 1850. Next to the nearby churchyard of St Mary's at Rydal is a field which Wordsworth bought to build a house when he thought he might have to leave Rydal Mount. But when his daughter Dora died in 1847, instead, he planted it with hundreds of daffodils in her memory. Today, Dora's Field, as it's known, is owned by the National Trust. Pay it a visit in daffodil or bluebell time.

Nab Cottage, tucked in under Nab Scar, had its own poetical connections. Thomas de Quincey lived there for a while and Hartley Coleridge, Samuel Taylor Coleridge's eldest son, died at Nab Cottage in 1849. Wordsworth always had a soft spot for the younger poet despite his wild ways and was at Hartley's bedside when he died.

But this is getting a bit sombre. Once you start the climb out to Nab Scar and start looking over your shoulder, as all fell walkers do when trying to pretend that they're not gasping for breath, you'll find an unfolding tapestry of delights. Rydal Water, opening out below you, captures and intensifies the light. On the other side of the lake there's the line of Loughrigg terrace meandering across the fell. It was set out on old quarry roads as a perfect stroll for Victorian ladies. Along the way they would brave a fit of the vapours as they passed the gaping maw of the Rydal Cave, a huge, echoing, hole in the ground carved out in the quest for quality slate. It's a dripping cathedral of rock, worth visiting in its own right, but we're getting the best distant view of it from the steep track out to Nab Scar.

But then, turning to look at our boot ends (Wainwright was very keen on boot ends: 'Watch where you're putting your feet' was his constant admonition), we come across an oddity. More or less at the point where Grasmere joins Rydal Water in the cabinet of beauties revealing themselves in views from the hill, we stumble across a blunt block of stone set into the ground. It marks the spot where the Thirlmere aqueduct, which supplies water to the Manchester conurbation, runs across the fell deep underground. There can be very few places where industry fits into the picturesque in quite such an understated way. But then you look up again into the blue grey distance and Windermere dominates the picture. And here Elterwater, and there Coniston. And a hint of Esthwaite Water, and a sparkle of Easedale Tarn. And you find yourself thinking, 'If the views are as good as this on a pimple above Rydal Water, why would anyone flog all the way round the Fairfield horseshoe?' But then, before you know it, you hear yourself saying, 'If the pictures are as good as this here, just imagine how much better they'll be from the top of Fairfield.'

And that's how the fell walking bug creeps into the system. And there's no known cure.

Descents
If you don't want to go down the same way, it's possible to descend via Alcock Tarn, and then return along the Coffin Route to Rydal, as detailed on the map on Nab Scar page 2.

Or – if you are feeling seriously energetic, have a copy of *The Eastern Fells*, and are properly equipped for a 12-mile walk over rough ground – you can take the ridge route to Heron Pike, as the next stage on the magnificent Fairfield Horseshoe!

Practical bits

Getting there
Rydal is between Ambleside and Grasmere on the A591.

Parking
There is space for parking on the road up to Rydal Mount and Rydal Hall from the A591, though it can fill up in the busy summer months. Pay via the honesty boxes. If space has run out, there is a car park at the western end of Rydal Water, further along the

A591 towards Grasmere – just under a mile's walk along a nice path to Rydal.

Public transport
The 555 Lakeslink bus service stops at Rydal every hour or so as it crosses the Lake District between north and south, linking Kendal, Windermere, Ambleside, Grasmere and Keswick, among other places. From mid March to late August, the 599 service calls at Rydal on its route between Windermere, Bowness, Ambleside and Grasmere.

General
If you are seeking refreshments before or after a walk, Rydal Hall has a good tea room, open daily all year round, and just off the A591 is the Glen Rothay Hotel and Badger Bar. For a greater choice of cafés, pubs, restaurants and shops, try Ambleside or Grasmere, a mile or two either side of Rydal on the A591.

Nab Scar 1450'

▲ FAIRFIELD

▲ GREAT RIGG

▲ STONE ARTHUR

▲ HERON PIKE

Grasmere ▲ NAB SCAR
• • Rydal

Ambleside •

MILES
0 1 2 3 4

from Rydal Water

NATURAL FEATURES

Nab Scar is well known. Its associations with the Lake Poets who came to dwell at the foot of its steep wooded slopes have invested it with romance, and its commanding position overlooking Rydal Water brings it to the notice of the many visitors to that charming lake. It is a fine abrupt height, with a rough, craggy south face; on the flanks are easier slopes. Elevated ground continues beyond the summit and rises gently to Heron Pike. Nab Scar is not a separate fell, but is merely the butt of the long southern ridge of Fairfield.

MAP

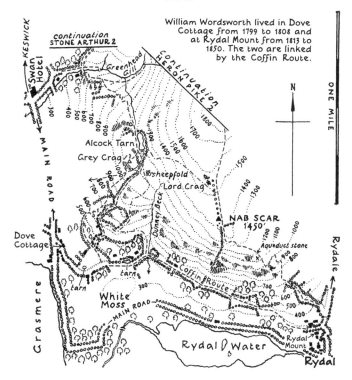

William Wordsworth lived in Dove Cottage from 1799 to 1808 and at Rydal Mount from 1813 to 1850. The two are linked by the Coffin Route.

ASCENTS

The popular ascent is from Rydal, a charming climb along a good path, steep in its middle reaches; this is the beginning of the 'Fairfield Horseshoe' when it is walked clockwise. Nab Scar can also be reached from the Swan Hotel by means of a path that rises from the south end of Alcock Tarn.

THE SUMMIT

Strictly, Nab Scar is the name of the craggy south face, not of the fell rising above it, but its recognised summit is a tall edifice of stones built well back from the edge of the cliffs, near a crumbled wall that runs north towards Heron Pike. Hereabouts the immediate surroundings are uninteresting, the redeeming feature being the fine view.

Nab Scar has a subterranean watercourse: below its surface the Thirlmere aqueduct runs through a tunnel. The scars of this operation are nearly gone, but evidence of the existence of the tunnel remains alongside the Rydal path, above the steepest part: here may be found a block of stone a yard square set in the ground; it bears no inscription but marks the position of the tunnel directly beneath.

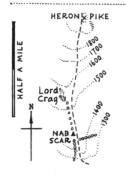

HERON PIKE
1800
1700
1600
1500
1400
1300
HALF A MILE
Lord
Crag
N
NAB
SCAR

RIDGE ROUTE

To HERON PIKE, 2008': ⅔ mile : N
570 feet of ascent
An easy climb on grass
A plain path accompanies the old wall, then it keeps to the right of the ridge.

THE VIEW

This is an 'unbalanced' view, most of it being exceptionally dull, the rest exceptionally charming. Lakes and tarns are a very special feature of the delightful prospect to south and west and the grouping of the Coniston and Langdale fells is quite attractive.

Principal Fells

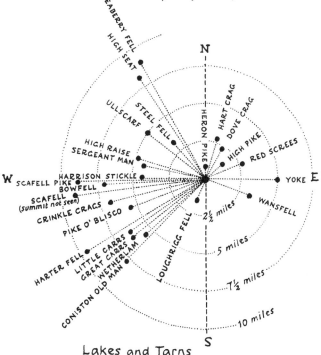

Lakes and Tarns

SSE	:	*Windermere*
S	:	*Blelham Tarn*
S	:	*Esthwaite Water*
SSW	:	*Coniston Water*
SW	:	*Elterwater*
WSW	:	*Grasmere*
WNW	:	*Easedale Tarn*
NW	:	*Alcock Tarn*

7 Orrest Head
from Windermere

Some of my most enjoyable excursions into the Lakeland hills have been in bits that Wainwright covered almost as an afterthought – the outlying fells. Maybe that's because the thought of ascents that can be done in carpet slippers gets more appealing as the years stumble on. AW listed all manner of reasons why people may turn to lesser hills – half a century of pipe-smoking, brittle bones, unsympathetic families, senile decay, sexual over-indulgence. As he said, though, 'Rigor mortis is the one great disability to fear, and avoid as long as possible.'

Assuming you have, and that the effects of the other little over-indulgences haven't taken too much of a toll, try the outlying fells and don't feel that you're giving in to failure.

When we began to film the 1990s television version of Wainwright's book – a series called *Remote Lakeland*, which took in a great circle of fells round the rim of the Lake District – I set out feeling that it was bound to be second division. We'd already ticked off the great summits in *Wainwright's Memorial Walk*, which revisited a route he'd devised in the 1930s for his mates in Blackburn town hall. After Scafell and Gable, Haystacks and Grasmoor, Bowfell and Blencathra, the outlying pimples (as I took to calling them) were bound to be a disappointment. How could Stickle Pike, Caw and Whitbarrow Scar possibly compete?

But they did, in great style. Being caught in low cloud on Whitbarrow Scar can be every bit as scary as being caught on Gable. There are still cliffs to fall over. Meanwhile, Caw offered an exposed climb and sparkling vistas that knock into a cocked hat the views from much bigger summits, and Stickle Pike is my favourite little mountain in the whole world. Yoadcastle was a lonely delight, Buck Barrow gave us the most theatrical meteorological moment, with double rainbows, a landscape of black and gold and rainstorms sweeping up the Irish Sea. And almost being blown off the Black Combe Screes sharpened up the intimations of mortality no end.

So how does Orrest Head fit into this beauty contest of lesser hills? Well, it seems to me that it misses out three times over. First, Wainwright popped it in with the outlying fells. Second, because it's so well known as AW's first view of Lakeland it has a 'been there, done that' feel to it. And third, it's a bit touristy and scruffy from overuse. All true but I'd still encourage you to go there because of its inspirational view.

Stand there where Wainwright stood that day in 1930 and if you're not knocked out by the panorama rolling away in front of you, rigor mortis has probably set in. Brim Fell to Steel Fell with the Scafells and Langdale Pikes in between. A place to inspire and draw you higher into the mountains or, if you're at the other end of the journey, a place to remember enjoyable days past when you used to indulge in grander, more energetic excursions.

Descents
If you don't want to go down the same way you came up, you have to continue north, as detailed on the

second page of Orrest Head, and return by way of the by-road and the footpath indicated.

Practical bits

Getting there and parking
Windermere gets very busy in the main summer months and parking space can sometimes be scarce. The main council facility is on Broad Street, and Booths supermarket has a big car park behind the railway station.

Given the weight of traffic in the town, it's a good idea to visit by public transport if you can. Wainwright arrived for his first walk up Orrest Head by bus, and there are plenty of services these days.

Public transport
The 555 Lakeslink bus service connects Carlisle in the north of Lakeland with Lancaster in the south, calling at Windermere railway station every hour or so daily. The 505 (Coniston), 516 (Langdale) and 519 (Kentmere) also run there, though services are less frequent in the winter, so contact Cumbria's Traveline for times and advice in advance (tel. 0871 200 22 33 or online at www.traveline.info).

Windermere is also the only town in the Lake District National Park that you can reach by train; a branch line connects you with Oxenholme, the main gateway to the Lakes on Virgin's west coast main line.

General
There are numerous cafés, pubs and restaurants to

choose from in Windermere's town centre (a short walk down the hill from the railway station), and more in Bowness. For picnic lunches, try Booths behind the station or other shops in the town.

Orrest Head
783'
400 feet of ascent

from WINDERMERE
RAILWAY STATION
2½ miles
2 hours
by the route described
1 mile : 1 hour
there and back direct

from the north

Orrest Head, for many of us, is "where we came in" — our first ascent in Lakeland, our first sight of mountains in tumultuous array across glittering waters, our awakening to beauty. It is a popular walk, deservedly, for here the promised land is seen in all its glory. It is a fitting finale, too, to a life made happy by fellwandering. Dare we hope there will be another Orrest Head over the threshold of the next heaven?

The way to Orrest Head is announced by a large signboard, which proclaims its unrivalled views and states that it is a twenty minutes' walk to the top. It is the leftmost of three drives that leave the main road opposite the bank close to the railway station, and is a tarmac strip initially. Almost at once a footpath goes off to the left: ignore this, keeping ahead and climbing gradually in a series of loops and bends. When a smithy is reached the path becomes rough; further, it divides into three branches: take the one on the right by a wall to reach and enter a fenced lane with many seats. This leads to a kissing gate; in the wall alongside is a memorial tablet to Arthur Henry Heywood, whose family gave Orrest Head for public enjoyment. Through the gate, and clear of trees at last, the view-indicator on the summit is seen on the left and soon reached. There is a choice of seats — iron, wood, stone and grass — from which to admire the fine view and reflect that, once upon a time, you too could have done this climb in twenty minutes just like that signboard said. Never mind. You've had a good innings.

Return the same way, or, if a longer alternative route is preferred, leave the rocky top by a path heading north to a quiet byroad, which follow left to join the A.592 road (to Troutbeck) but without actually setting foot on it go through a gate on the left (public footpath sign), whence a good path leads forward into a wood and continues very pleasantly past some handsome residences amid noble trees, rejoining the outward route only a few paces from the starting point: in fact along the path ignored earlier.

There is room to park on the Kendal road just past the de-restriction sign.

The view indicator on the summit

The indicator was replaced in 2002, but by 2008 was already showing signs of damage.

MAP

HALF A MILE

Windermere

THE VIEW

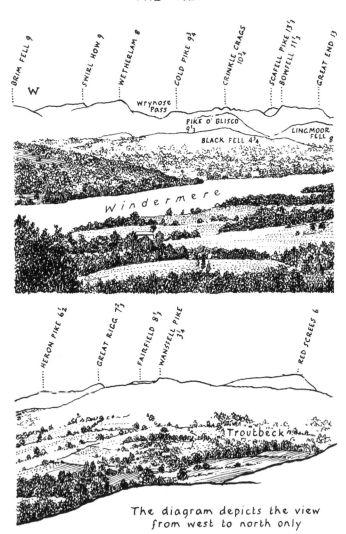

BRIM FELL 9
W
SWIRL HOW 9
WETHERLAM 8
COLD PIKE 9¾
Wrynose Pass
CRINKLE CRAGS 10¼
SCAFELL PIKE 11½
BOWFELL 13½
GREAT END 13
PIKE O' BLISCO 9⅓
LING.MOOR FELL 8
BLACK FELL 4¾

Windermere

HERON PIKE 6½
GREAT RIGG 7¾
FAIRFIELD 8½
WANSFELL PIKE 3¾
RED SCREES 6

Troutbeck

The diagram depicts the view
from west to north only

THE VIEW

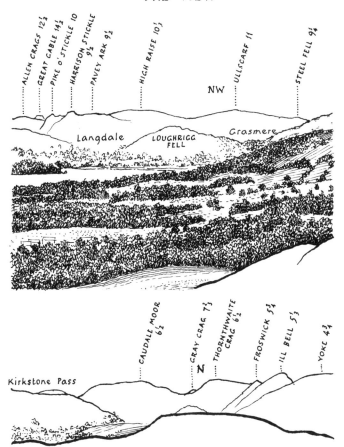

ALLEN CRAGS 12½
GREAT GABLE 14½
PIKE o'STICKLE 10
HARRISON STICKLE 9½
PAVEY ARK 9½
HIGH RAISE 10½
NW
ULLSCARF 11
STEEL FELL 9½

Langdale   LOUGHRIGG FELL   Grasmere

CAUDALE MOOR 6½
GRAY CRAG 7¾
THORNTHWAITE CRAG 6½
FROSWICK 5¾
ILL BELL 5⅓
YOKE 4¾

N

Kirkstone Pass

The thick line is the outline of the summit rocks.

The figures accompanying the names of fells
indicate distances in miles.

Summit seats and litter, which occur in profusion,
and the view indicator, are omitted.

8 Place Fell
from Patterdale

Wainwright reckoned that the path alongside Ullswater, rounding the northern end of Place Fell, was the most beautiful in all Lakeland. Now, I know we've all got our own candidates for that coveted award – mine would be closer to Wastwater than Ullswater – but AW's choice should be enough to tempt you to the area. And the ascent of Place Fell that's on offer in this podcast will set the seal on a great day out. Guaranteed. It's an ascent to savour and remember long after the images of excursions onto better-known summits have faded.

What makes this trip so special is that there's never an unattractive moment. With so many of the big ascents, before you get to the promised land there's a flog up a dreary track which may be good for the soul but is decidedly lacking in the senses department. But this expedition onto Place Fell gives you views from the off. As AW reported in *Wainwright's Lakeland*:

> The views on this ascent are of superlative beauty. Ahead is Brothers Water and Kirkstone Pass, deep-set amongst encroaching heights; behind is a glorious prospect of the Patterdale Valley with the massive bulk of the Helvellyn range towering towards the deep trench of Grisedale. Ullswater completes a delightful picture.

It's 2154 feet to the Place Fell summit and every foot of the way offers a kaleidoscope of shifting back-drops. In golden sunburst or under lowering skies they're enough to take your breath away. It's also one of those places that help to explain the complex topography of Lakeland; how the valleys interlock in the jigsaw of the mountains. Boredale Hause is, as Wainwright describes it, a walkers' crossroads with tracks heading for Mardale and Martindale and Boredale itself. Tempting excursions for another day.

You might think that the views are just so good on the way up that, once you get to the top, it's bound be an anticlimax. But it's not. Once you're out there among the tarns on the summit, you'll find it hard to drag yourself away as you take out your, by now, well-thumbed copy of this book and try to identify the fifty or so summits arrayed around you. Loadpot Hill to Gowbarrow Fell, Wether Hill to Caudale Moor, Red Screes to Whiteside, Great Mell Fell to Raise. And, yes that has to be Striding Edge and could that be a hint of Clough Head below Skiddaw? And away to the north, tantalising views into the Scottish Borders, and to the north-east, the Pennines running out to Cross Fell.

Place Fell demonstrates perfectly what a contained little place the Lake District is. How accessible. How beckoning. I bet you have a dozen new expeditions planned by the time you retrace your steps to Boredale Hause. And on the way down, reflect on the fact that you're walking through a landscape that's been home and workplace and destination of choice to people for hundreds of years. People who, like you, have looked out from the summit of Place Fell and marvelled. Others who have travelled these mountain tracks with their flocks of Herdwick sheep or the tools of the quarryman. Others still who have made their way out of the valley to worship at the little ruined chapel on the Hause. Stop there for a moment's reflection on the way down.

Descents
If you don't want to go back the same way you came up, the best route down is to Sandwick. (See Place Fell page 6 for the details, and pages 3–4 for a map.) You can then either walk back to Patterdale on the path along the shores of Ullswater, described by Wainwright as 'the most beautiful and rewarding walk in Lakeland' or walk on to Howtown pier and take the almost equally rewarding steamer ride back to Glenridding, whence it is a short road walk to Patterdale.

Practical bits

Getting there
Access to Patterdale is via the A592, crossing the dramatic Kirkstone Pass if you are arriving from the south.

Parking
There is one car park in the village, well signed from the A592. There are also a few free roadside spaces, though you will have to arrive early in the day to find them empty.

Public transport
From the north, the 108 Patterdale Bus picks up every

few hours at Penrith, Pooley Bridge and Glenridding on the way to the Patterdale Hotel; the 208 Ullswater Connexion runs there from Keswick on weekends and Bank Holidays between late May and the end of August only. From the south, the 517 Kirkstone Rambler service links Bowness and Windermere with Patterdale three times a day on weekends and Bank Holidays from March to November, and daily in the school summer holidays.

The Ullswater Steamers (telephone 017684 82229 or online www.ullswater-steamers.co.uk) run all the year round between Pooley Bridge, Howtown and Glenridding.

General

There are a couple of hotels in Patterdale that serve food, and there are more a mile or so up the A592 in Glenridding. Patterdale also has a very good village store that will equip you with food for a picnic. including home-made bread. It is open every day in summer, but closes on Wednesday and Sunday afternoons in winter.

Place Fell

2154'

from Birks

Howtown •

▲ PLACE FELL

• Patterdale

MILES
0   1   2   3

Few fells are so well favoured as Place Fell for appraising neighbouring heights. It occupies an exceptionally good position in the curve of Ullswater, in the centre of a great bowl of hills; its summit commands a very beautiful and impressive panorama. On a first visit to Patterdale, Place Fell should be an early objective, for no other viewpoint gives such an appreciation of the design of this lovely corner of Lakeland.

NATURAL FEATURES

Place Fell rises steeply from the curve formed by the upper and middle reaches of Ullswater and its bulky mass dominates the head of the lake. Of only moderate elevation, and considerably overtopped by surrounding heights, nevertheless the fell more than holds its own even in such a goodly company: it has that distinctive blend of outline and rugged solidity characteristic of the true mountain. Many discoveries await those who explore: in particular the abrupt western flank, richly clothed with juniper and bracken and heather, and plunging down to the lake in a rough tumble of crag and scree, boulders and birches, is a paradise for the scrambler, while a more adventurous walker will find a keen enjoyment in tracing the many forgotten and overgrown paths across the fellside and in following the exciting and airy sheep-tracks that so skilfully contour the steep upper slopes below the hoary crest.

The eastern face, overlooking Boredale, is riven by deepcut gullies and is everywhere steep. Northward two ridges descend more gradually to the shores of Ullswater after passing over minor summits; from a lonely hollow between them issues the main stream on the fell, Scalehow Beck, which has good waterfalls. To the south, Boredale Hause is a well-known walkers' crossroads, and beyond this depression high ground continues to climb towards the principal watershed.

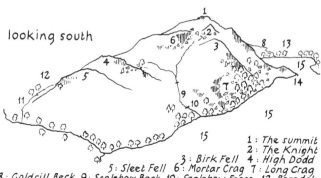

looking south

1 : The summit
2 : The Knight
3 : Birk Fell   4 : High Dodd
5 : Sleet Fell 6 : Mortar Crag 7 : Long Crag
8 : Goldrill Beck 9 : Scalehow Beck 10 : Scalehow Force 12 : Boredale
11 : Boredale Beck 13 : Patterdale 14 : Silver Point 15 : Ullswater

MAP

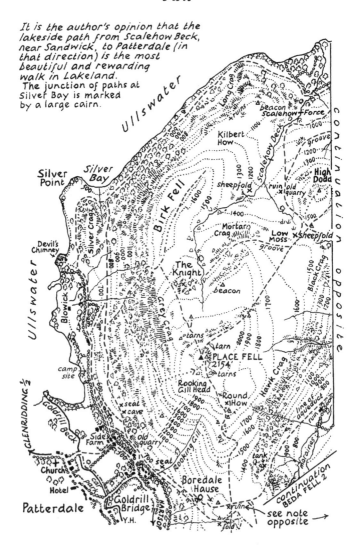

It is the author's opinion that the lakeside path from Scalehow Beck, near Sandwick, to Patterdale (in that direction) is the most beautiful and rewarding walk in Lakeland.
The junction of paths at Silver Bay is marked by a large cairn.

MAP

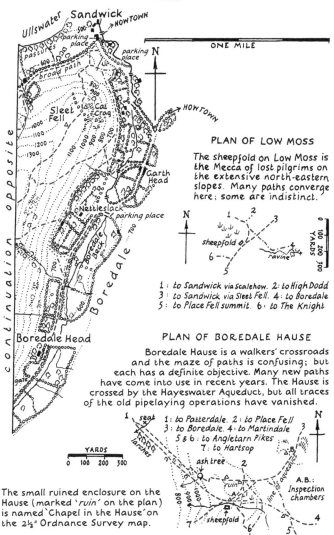

ONE MILE

PLAN OF LOW MOSS

The sheepfold on Low Moss is the Mecca of lost pilgrims on the extensive north-eastern slopes. Many paths converge here; some are indistinct.

1 : to Sandwick via Scalehow. 2 : to High Dodd
3 : to Sandwick via Sleet Fell. 4 : to Boredale
5 : to Place Fell summit. 6 : to The Knight

PLAN OF BOREDALE HAUSE

Boredale Hause is a walkers' crossroads and the maze of paths is confusing; but each has a definite objective. Many new paths have come into use in recent years. The Hause is crossed by the Hayeswater Aqueduct, but all traces of the old pipelaying operations have vanished.

1 : to Patterdale. 2 : to Place Fell
3 : to Boredale. 4 : to Martindale
5 & 6 : to Angletarn Pikes
7 : to Hartsop

A.B. : Inspection chambers

YARDS
0   100   200   300

The small ruined enclosure on the Hause (marked 'ruin' on the plan) is named 'Chapel in the Hause' on the 2½" Ordnance Survey map.

ASCENT FROM PATTERDALE
1700 feet of ascent : 1¾ miles

The face of Place Fell overlooking Patterdale is unremittingly and uncompromisingly steep, and the ascent is invariably made by way of the easier gradients of Boredale Hause, there being a continuous path on this route. (*From the valley there appear to be paths going straight up the fell, but these are not paths at all: they are incipient streams and runnels.*) As an alternative, an old neglected track that branches from the higher path to Silver Bay is recommended: this slants leftwards to the skyline depression between Birk Fell and Grey Crag. This old track is difficult to locate from above and is better not used for descent as there is rough ground in the vicinity.

The diversion of the old track from the higher path to Silver Bay occurs a full half-mile beyond the quarry at a point where there is a bluff of grey rock on the left above some larches. A flat boulder marks the junction, and a few ancient cairns along the route are also a help. Botanists will find much of interest here.

Note also, 200 yards up the old track, a faint path turning away on the right: this climbs high across the face below Grey Crag, is lost on scree, but can be traced beyond, on the 1500' contour, all the way to the usual route *via* Boredale Hause—an exhilarating high-level walk. From this path the summit may be gained without difficulty *after* leaving Grey Crag behind and crossing a small ravine.

On the Boredale Hause route, take the upper path at the fork near the seat. Watch for the zig-zag: if this is missed the walker naturally gravitates to the lower path. The striking ash tree is on the *upper* path.

One cannot sojourn at Patterdale without looking at Place Fell and one cannot look long at Place Fell without duly setting forth to climb it. The time is very well spent.

ASCENT FROM SANDWICK
1700 feet of ascent : 2½ miles

Of the two routes shown from
Low Moss to the summit,
the one on the left
is *very much*
the better.

PLACE FELL

Top of Grey Crag

The Knight

grass beacon

Mortar Crag

Low Moss sheepfold

Birk Fell

grass sheepfold

High Dodd ruin

Scalehow Beck

beacon

BOREDALE HAUSE

ravine

groove

Sleet Fell old wall

←path choked with bracken in summer

Scalehow Force

PATTERDALE 3

bracken

barn

Nettleslack

barn

←path starts 70 yards past double bend in wall

barn

Boredale Beck

bracken

Ullswater

seat broad path

HOWTOWN 1½

parking place Sandwick Beck

signpost

parking place

Sandwick

HOWTOWN 1¾

looking south-west

Five alternatives are shown
for the initial part of the climb,
the best on a clear day being over
the top of Sleet Fell (which is steep).
All ways converge near the sheepfold on
Low Moss, beyond which is a further choice.

- -

THE SUMMIT

A rocky ridge overtops gently-rising
slopes and has a cairn at one end and
a triangulation column at the other.
There is a better cairn farther north.

DESCENTS : Routes of descent are indicated in the illustration
of the view; that to Boredale Hause is safest in bad weather.

THE VIEW

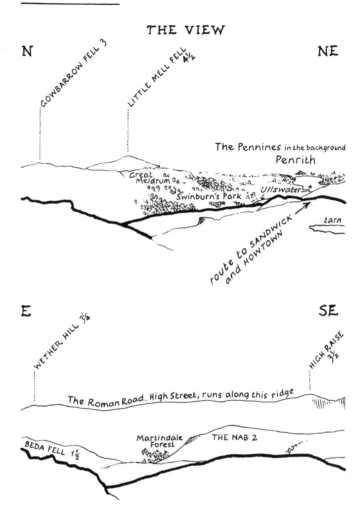

N

GOWBARROW FELL 3

LITTLE MELL FELL 4½

NE

The Pennines in the background
Penrith

Great
Meldrum

Swinburn's Park

Ullswater

route to SANDWICK
and HOWTOWN

tarn

E

WETHER HILL 3¾

SE

HIGH RAISE 3½

The Roman Road, High Street, runs along this ridge

BEDA FELL 1½

Martindale
Forest

THE NAB 2

The thick line marks the visible boundaries
of Place Fell from the summit cairn.
   The figures following the names of fells
   indicate distances in miles.

THE VIEW

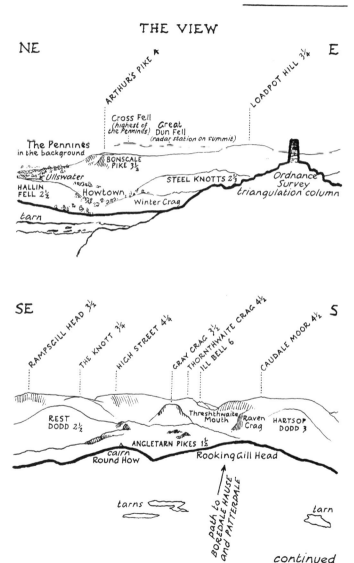

NE

ARTHUR'S PIKE ↖

Cross Fell
(highest of
the Pennines)

Great
Dun Fell
(radar station on summit)

LOADPOT HILL 3¼

E

The Pennines
in the background

BONSCALE
PIKE 3½

Ullswater

STEEL KNOTTS 2½

Ordnance
Survey
triangulation column

HALLIN
FELL 2½

Howtown

Winter Crag

tarn

SE

RAMPSGILL HEAD 3½

THE KNOTT 3¼

HIGH STREET 4¼

GRAY CRAG 3½

THORNTHWAITE CRAG 4½

ILL BELL 6

CAUDALE MOOR 4½

S

REST
DODD 2½

Threshthwaite
Mouth

Raven
Crag

HARTSOP
DODD 3

ANGLETARN PIKES 1½

cairn
Round How

Rooking Gill Head

PATH TO
BOREDALE HAUSE
AND PATTERDALE

tarns

tarn

continued

THE VIEW

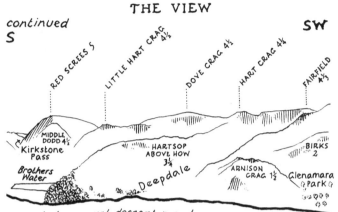

continued S

SW

RED SCREES S · LITTLE HART CRAG 4½ · DOVE CRAG 4½ · HART CRAG 4¾ · FAIRFIELD 4⅔

MIDDLE DODD 4½
Kirkstone Pass
Brothers Water

HARTSOP ABOVE HOW 3½

Deepdale

ARNISON CRAG 1½

BIRKS 2

Glenamara Park

A steep, rough descent may be made to Patterdale over this edge, but there is no path. The Boredale Hause route is to be preferred, and takes no longer

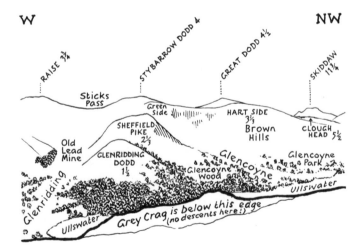

W

NW

RAISE 3¾ · STYBARROW DODD 4 · GREAT DODD 4½ · SKIDDAW 11¾

Sticks Pass

Green Side

HART SIDE 3⅓
Brown Hills

CLOUGH HEAD 5½

Old Lead Mine

SHEFFIELD PIKE 2⅔

GLENRIDDING DODD 1½

Glencoyne
Glencoyne Wood

Glencoyne Park

Glenridding

Ullswater

Ullswater

Grey Crag is below this edge (no descents here!)

THE VIEW

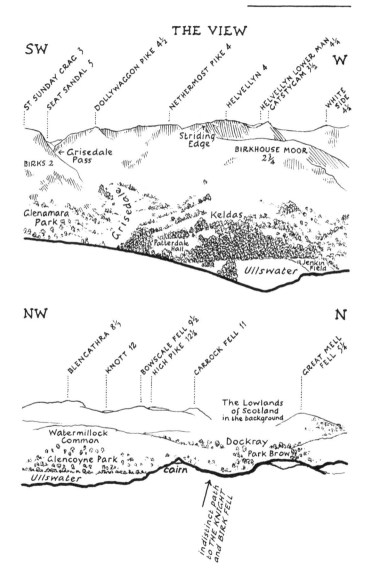

Safety Note

Fell walking can be **dangerous**.

Before setting out :
– Consult an up-to-date map showing all of the route you plan to take.
– Study the relevant Wainwright Pictorial Guide, taking note of any suggestions, difficulties or warnings associated with your route. (For the most up-to-date information, use the Second Edition.)
– Some walks are more challenging than others. Assess the length and difficulty of your route and make sure you, and any walkers with you, are physically and mentally fit enough to complete it in daylight.
– Check the weather forecast: ring 0870 0550575 for forecasts for the Lake District or visit www.lake district.gov.uk/weatherline. Even an easy walk can become dangerous in wet, windy, misty or icy weather.
– Wear appropriate footgear and clothing for the conditions and the terrain. Weather can change quickly: take waterproof outerwear and spare warm clothes.
– Make sure you have the equipment you need, including your map, a compass, a torch and a whistle (to signal in an emergency).
– Pack enough in the way of snacks and water for the expedition.
– Tell someone where you are going, the route you plan to take, and when you expect to return. Then they can raise the alarm if you do not reappear as expected.

When out on the fells:
– Be prepared to cut short or abandon your walk if conditions worsen.
– Use your common sense at all times.
– Watch where you are putting your feet.

These safety points are only a start. You should visit the website for the Mountain Rescue Council on www.mountain.rescue.org.uk for further guidance on safety on the fells.

Every care has been taken to ensure the accuracy of this guide. However, the publishers do not accept liability for any harm, injury, damage or loss a walker may sustain when following any of the routes included in this volume.